TESTIMONY
BY
FIRE

Also by Atulya Misra

Oxygen Manifesto: A Battle for the Environment

Vultures of Paradise

TESTIMONY BY FIRE

ATULYA MISRA

RUPA

Published by
Rupa Publications India Pvt. Ltd 2025
161-B/4, Gulmohar House,
Yusuf Sarai Community Centre,
New Delhi 110049

Sales centres:
Bengaluru Chennai
Hyderabad Kolkata Mumbai

Copyright © Atulya Misra 2025

P-ISBN: 978-93-7003-948-3
E-ISBN: 978-93-7003-954-4

First impression 2025

10 9 8 7 6 5 4 3 2 1

The moral right of the author has been asserted.

Printed in India

To India's freedom fighters—
with deepest reverence and enduring gratitude.

To
my grandfather, the late Bhogilal,
my grandmother, the late Premvati,
my maternal grandfather, the late Radha Charan,
my father, Dr Sarvadaman,
and my aunt, the late Dr Veena—
whose sacrifices in the struggle for independence
and tireless efforts in building the nation
continue to illuminate my path
and inspire every word of this work.

∞

Contents

Prologue   *ix*

1. Whispers from the Hills   3

2. Carrying Many Skies   10

3. Seasons of Stillness   18

4. The Fire That Would Not Burn   26

5. The Ghost Who Walked   30

6. The Jungle That Raised Him   41

7. The Boy with a Hundred Names   53

8. The Flames of Fate   65

9. The Truth beneath the Smoke   76

10. The Crown of Courage   86

11. Ashes of Glory   94

12. Between the Squares of Silence   101

13. The Accidental President   112

14. The Silent Head of State   117

15. The Quiet Crusader   126

16. The Endless March   136

17. Where Guns Grew from Dust   147

18. The Silence That Walked Through Kashi   154

19. The Eyes That Did Not Look Away   165

20. The Barefoot Saint in Sikkim   172

21. A City of Shadows and Shine   180

22. Beaches, Bells and Broken Promises   187

23. The Silent Steps to Bodh Gaya   194

24. Flowing Through India's Sacred Heart   199

25. Echoes of Faith and Fragile Waters   207

26. Through the Shadows of a Changing Land   214

27. The Last Cry beneath the Lone Pine   221

Epilogue   229

Acknowledgements   230

Prologue

In the beginning, there was dust.
And silence.
And a man who rose from the ashes of his own ending.

He walked without destination,
barefoot across the bruised skin of a wounded land,
carrying no flag,
no gospel,
no command.

He did not speak.
Yet the earth heard him.
The rivers trembled at his passing.
The forgotten people found their voices in his silence.

This is not a tale of conquest.
This is not a story of crowns or victories.
It is the testimony of a soul set aflame—
And the land that bore witness.

Follow, if you wish.
But know this:
You will not return the same.

ATULYA MISRA

Part One

Chapter 1

Whispers from the Hills

In the hilly terrains of Arunachal Pradesh, a state nestled in the north-eastern fringes of the Indian Republic, a tale of legacy and ambition was about to unfold.

My story begins with my grandfather, Tashi Dorjee, the Grambodha (a kind of village chieftain) of a village near Bomdila. He was stout and well built, his face sharp and weathered like the cliffs around us. His small, bright eyes always watched, always thought. He wore a red yak-wool coat with tribal patterns and turquoise beads passed down from his forefathers. His voice rumbled deep and slow, and when he spoke, Bomdila listened.

His village was small, comprising stone and bamboo houses with sloping roofs, smoke curling from chimneys and prayer flags flapping in the wind. Beyond, the hills stretched wild, hiding deer, black bears, bison, apes and even leopards.

The Grambodha was more than a leader; he was a lifeline. Even after India's independence, when a democratic government took over, his role held strong. Grandfather was the bridge linking our Monpa tribe to the outside world, which barely noticed us. While the rest of the world may have overlooked Arunachal Pradesh, its people thrived, holding on to traditions more ancient than the map itself.

As Grambodha, he had no office. He walked Bomdila's dirt paths, tapping his staff, settling disputes with words, brewing herbal tea for the sick, lighting butter lamps for lost souls. Although the roots of Tibetan Buddhism influenced our ancestors, they did not strictly adhere to religious practices. Instead, their faith resonated more with nature worship. Our beliefs lived in the land—in its rivers, trees and sky—not just in temples. The Tawang Monastery's chants echoed across the hills, but the Grambodha was our true guide. He was an ambassador, forging links between our secluded world and the vastness beyond.

I never lived with my grandfather, but I feel him in my bones—like unseen roots. My father, Otem Dorjee, told me his tales. Father was taller, thinner, quieter—his face softer, eyes wide and curious behind slipping glasses, hands stained with ink. He was the first to leave the hills, thanks to Grandfather's bold decision.

Missionaries brought modern education to the frontier.

A British officer, Captain Harrow, came to Bomdila—a wiry man with a broom-like moustache and a barking laugh. He was mapping the hills for the Empire when he met Grandfather and saw his wisdom. 'Send your son to school,' he said. 'The future's coming fast.'

Grandfather did not trust the British, but he trusted learning. So, at ten, Father trekked to Itanagar. It took him weeks—rickety bridges, starry nights, carrying rice, a blanket, and a letter. Itanagar was louder, dustier, with brick houses and the wide Dihang river nearby. He learnt English, mathematics and history. His Dakpa accent faded as he topped his class.

Father's thirst for knowledge grew. He took a rattling bus to Guwahati—Assam's bustling heart. The markets were loud, fish and spices thickened the air, and the Brahmaputra cut through the city. He stayed in a leaky hostel, but his academic prowess earned him a scholarship to the esteemed St Xavier's College in Calcutta.

That city was a furnace. Trams clanged, the Hooghly river shimmered, the crowd, the faces—all so different from his remote village. St Xavier's was grand: red-brick walls, arched windows, Jesuit teachers. My father pursued Political Science for his master's. Under banyan trees, he scribbled dreams of change. Calcutta forged him into becoming an officer of the Indian Administrative

Service (IAS), the first from Arunachal.

However, the India–China conflict shadowed Father's life. In 1950, China annexed Tibet, ending its role as a buffer. The Dalai Lama fled to India through Tawang, welcomed by the people of Arunachal, which enraged China. Then came 1962. During the Sino-Indian war, Chinese troops stormed into Arunachal, capturing Tawang and Bomdila, reaching as far as Tezpur. India lost huge chunks of land in Aksai Chin, and thousands perished. Though China withdrew from Arunachal after a ceasefire, the wound remained. China kept calling Arunachal 'South Tibet', renaming places and building villages near the Line of Actual Control—a fuzzy border neither side fully accepts.

My mother, Hema, came from Kanchipuram in Tamil Nadu, a town of silk and temples. Tamil life was old and rich: temple bells at dawn, *kolams* drawn with rice flour, prayers to Shiva and Vishnu. Meals were idlis and dosas with tangy sambar on banana leaves. Pongal brought sweet rice and harvest songs. Her family lived by Tamil hymns and Sanskrit chants.

She studied at Loyola College in Madras. It was a grand white building surrounded by coconut and palm trees and had a chapel with stained glass on its campus. My mother loved its large library full of books. With a soft Tamil accent and quiet fire, she qualified for the IAS and joined the so-called elite.

My parents met at the IAS Academy in Mussoorie,

nestled in the Himalayas. Cool air and pine slopes framed the Lal Bahadur Shastri Academy, where trainees drilled on wet lawns and debated over pakoras and tea. Father's Monpa calm met Mother's Tamil spark. Their love began on a trek to the Rupin Pass, a high trail between Garhwal and Himachal Pradesh, designed to test their grit.

After a brief courtship they got married in an Arya Samaj temple. Later they visited the Tibetan monastery at Majnu ka Tila in Delhi and received the blessings of a monk before registering themselves as man and wife.

The reactions of the traditional Grambodha from Arunachal Pradesh and the Tamils of Kanchipuram to this union remained a mystery. It was a topic conspicuously absent from household conversations. By the time I became aware of my surroundings, we had settled in Madhya Pradesh. My maternal grandmother lived with us. My maternal grandfather had passed away before my parents' wedding. The Grambodha, my paternal grandmother, and the clan from my father's side never embarked on the arduous journey to visit us. They remained deeply rooted in their homeland, surrounded by kin and familiar terrains, choosing to thrive, and ultimately rest, among their ancestors.

The IAS defined my parents' life. What began as the Indian Civil Service to govern an empire evolved into the IAS to build a nation. Officers like my parents oversaw districts of about two million people, managing schools, hospitals, floods and riots, their lives uprooted with each posting, their hours stretching late into the night.

A typical district officer's day began early. At six in the morning, they would rise, sip tea while poring over reports on crop yields, road repairs and schools without roofs. By seven-thirty, they would be in the office—a dusty room with a creaky fan and files stacked high. Villagers lined up outside: farmers with land disputes and complaints of encroachments, women seeking ration cards. Each grievance met with a patient ear, pen scribbling orders, voice calling officials to act. Evenings brought more petitions and paperwork, the day finally ending past nine—tired but resolute, they served India one steady task at a time. The IAS was India's glue, often stretched thin.

Summer vacations occasionally brought the adventure of visiting my grandparents. It involved a long train journey from Delhi to Guwahati, followed by a helicopter ride to Itanagar, and then a combination of pony rides and walking. Often, by the time we arrived, it was nearly time to return due to my parents' tight work schedules. But what I vividly recall was the close-knit community, where everyone was kin, where joys, sorrows and resources were shared. However, over time, these visits dwindled.

My grandfather died early, leaving Nima, my tiny

grandmother, in Bomdila, weaving and singing Dakpa lullabies. Mother's stern mother, Lavanya, lived with us in Madhya Pradesh, cooking *rasam* and praying in Tamil. Her ancestral house in Kanchipuram had a red-tiled roof amid wheat fields and mango trees. I grew up between two worlds: Arunachal's wild hills and Tamil Nadu's sacred plains. Father taught me Dakpa and Assamese; Mother and Lavanya, Tamil. Moreover, Hindi and English fitted the outside world. I carried my mixed lineage with pride—a unique genome, a distinct appearance.

When my parents were transferred to Delhi, their responsibilities magnified. The civil services became an all-consuming career, often placing them in separate cities. This constant shuffle and their dedication to their professions meant I remained an only child.

This tale starts here, a thread through time. But the real story waits—someone who will shift it all. For now, I hold these roots: rough, beautiful and, above all, mine.

Chapter 2

Carrying Many Skies

My life in Delhi began to take shape when we moved there from Madhya Pradesh. The city was a whirlwind—cars honking, streets buzzing, the stone arch of India Gate glowing at night near our new home. I studied at St Columba's School, a place of red-brick walls and strict teachers in white cassocks. The classrooms smelled of chalk and old wood, and the playground echoed with boys shouting over cricket matches. I was quiet, my mixed Monpa–Tamil features drawing curious stares, but I found my place among books and history lessons.

Later, I joined St Stephen's College to study history. The college was grand, with green lawns, arched corridors and students debating under neem trees. History pulled me in, stories of kings and borders, like those that shaped Arunachal Pradesh, my father's home.

In Delhi, my parents grew into new roles. Father became a guardian for students from the Northeast—boys and girls from Arunachal, Assam, Manipur—helping them find hostels, navigate exams or simply feel less alone in the big city. His gentle Monpa ways made him a steady hand for them. Mother got involved with Tamil Sanghams, cultural groups where women in silk saris sang old songs and planned festivals like Pongal and Karthika deepam. She would come home with stories of temple dances and the smell of jasmine in her hair. Their IAS lives kept them busy; they often toured separately—Father to drought-affected regions, fixing water shortages, Mother to flooded districts, arranging rescue and relief. But Delhi was our anchor at that time.

The two religions of my birth—Buddhism and Hinduism—lived quietly side by side in me. Father's Monpa roots tied me to Tibetan Buddhism with prayer flags and butter lamps. Mother's Tamil lineage brought Hindu rituals, kolams and temple bells. They did not clash; they simply coexisted, like the hills and plains I came from. Yet I lived afar from religion, much like my grandfather in Arunachal's deep valleys. When I visited a monastery, a temple, or even the school church, I stood back, watching—not praying. Religion was distant, something I observed with neutrality, neither for nor against. I was not an atheist, just non-religious, flowing with it all. Sometimes I was

Buddhist, sometimes Hindu, mostly neither.

Respecting my parents' aspirations, I attempted the civil services examinations and secured a commendable rank. They sat me down one evening—Father with his slipping glasses, Mother with her sharp eyes—and said the Indian Foreign Service (IFS) would suit me best.

'You are calm; you adapt,' Father said.

'It fits your temperament,' Mother added.

I joined the IFS, a world of embassies and borders, but my entry sparked a protest from China. They claimed Arunachal Pradesh as their own, calling it an 'integral part of China', and declared that I was a Chinese citizen. It was then that I felt a profound connection to my ancestral roots and to the Grambodha.

My first posting was to Vietnam—a land of green rice fields and humid air. I landed in Hanoi; the embassy was a squat building with flaking paint. I started learning the Vietnamese language—its sharp tones and quick words tangled my tongue. IFS life was a rush from day one. There were trade meetings with exporters, visa queues to manage, weekly reports typed on a clunky machine and sent to New Delhi via Air India in envelopes marked confidential.

As fate would have it, love blossomed in the most unexpected of places. I met her at an Osho meditation centre, a quiet room filled with incense and soft chants. Her name was Linh, a Vietnamese girl with dark eyes and a gentle laugh. We sat cross-legged, eyes closed, breathing together. She saw past my odd mix of Monpa and Tamil; I saw her calm strength. We married in a simple ceremony. Her family attended in silk *ao dais*; mine sent blessings from Delhi. Our union was a wild blend—animism from her village, Tibetan Buddhism and Hinduism from mine, even traces of Chinese Buddhism from her roots. Osho's teachings held us: aloof yet spiritual, meditative, observant, not bound by routine prayers. I loved her deeply, her hand in mine a steady warmth.

The diplomat's life pulled us across continents, a roller-coaster of postings with no warning. In Kenya, I served as a junior officer in Nairobi. The city sprawled under acacia trees, red dust coating my shoes. I negotiated coffee exports, met Maasai traders in bright *shukas*, hosted dusty receptions where diplomats sweated in suits. Linh loved the savannah—wide skies, giraffes in the distance—but the heat wore her down.

Then came Bolivia, South America. La Paz sat high in the Andes, the air so thin we gasped at first. I worked on lithium deals, trudged up steep streets to meet miners, wrote reports at 3,600 metres above sea level. Linh struggled with the altitude, her face pale, but she painted the mountains with her brush.

Uncertainty was part of the job. One year we would settle; the next, we would pack again. Orders from New Delhi were abrupt and final.

Our assignments spanned the globe, with short

stints back in New Delhi offering moments of respite. Once, I took on the role of Regional Passport Officer in Chennai, hoping to connect more deeply with my maternal relatives, most of whom still lived in what was formerly known as Madras State.

In India, my appearance and heritage often piqued curiosity. But abroad, distinctions faded. We were universally seen as Indians. Even my Vietnamese wife, in the eyes of the world, was Indian. There were no probing questions or lingering doubts. To them, being Indian was not just about looks but a myriad of experiences, traditions and values. As a family, we embodied that essence.

Our lives split between postings, my parents' house in Delhi and Linh's village in North Vietnam—a cluster of wooden homes by a river, her parents smiling under straw hats. We travelled through the misty hills of Bomdila and to Kanchipuram, my mother's temple town of silk and chants. Our two daughters grew up between these places, absorbing lullabies in different tongues, learning to fold their hands in greeting in three different ways.

As I ascended in my career, life's inevitable ebb made its presence felt. Mornings often began with news of an elderly relative's passing in Bomdila; by evening, I would hear of another loss from Chennai. The rituals became all too familiar—drafting a message of condolence or making a heartfelt phone call. My visits to Bomdila and

Kanchipuram seemed increasingly confined to attending funerals. Time wore on, and soon my parents became my last living connection to my roots.

And then tragedy struck.

Linh went to her village during a tense period when Vietnam's borders were simmering with conflict. She wanted to see her ageing parents. A bombardment hit and her village was burned to ashes. I waited, heart pounding, believing she had escaped. My diplomatic channels stretched thin, chasing leads through consulates, non-government organizations, local contacts…nothing.

For years, I clung to hope that she had slipped away, healthy and smiling. Finally, I went there alone; the land was black and silent. I scooped a handful of scorched earth from where her house once stood, carried it to Rameswaram, and immersed it in the sea, reciting farewell prayers through tears. She was gone. A void I could not fill. I felt her absence like a missing limb. I longed for her laugh, her touch, the way she hummed Osho chants. I flowed on, detached and broken.

Our daughters, meanwhile, pursued their studies at American schools wherever we were posted. In time, they made their way to renowned universities in the United States. Life unfolded for them; the elder found love with a classmate in Texas, the younger with a Cambodian colleague.

Back in India, the foreign services took me far. I

eventually became External Affairs Secretary, overseeing ambassadors, treaties and crises. But a new government abruptly reshuffled positions. Someone else needed the Foreign Secretary post, and luck made me Secretary to the President when an IAS colleague became Home Secretary.

I landed in Rashtrapati Bhavan, serving His Excellency Ranji—a medium-built, dark and balding man with a flowing beard like a sage's. He was in his last months in office as the presidential elections were looming.

We clicked instantly—two men at the end of their careers, staring down retirement's quiet horizon.

Those months were slow. Few visitors. No foreign tours. Only occasional ceremonies. We would sit in his office, looking vaguely at marble floors and high ceilings, sipping tea and talking about life beyond titles. Ranji shared stories of his village; I told him about Linh, the hills, the various postings. We were preparing to leave; the world waiting for new faces.

After superannuation, I stored my things in a godown at the National Academy and began hunting for a rental in the National Capital Region (NCR) suburbs.

Later, I read in the newspapers that the new President had taken office. Ranji had moved to a bungalow in Lutyens' Delhi, living simply with modest perks.

I travelled to the United States. My journey took me to Chicago, then to Los Angeles, reuniting me with my daughters. The initial novelty of a carefree existence devoid of the routine nine-to-five grind was invigorating. But as days merged into weeks, I sensed my daughters' comfort in their nuclear family dynamics. While my occasional visits were warmly received, my continuous presence seemed to intrude on their established lives. Although not unexpected, this new scenario was not palatable. A longing for personal space and freedom, combined with certain ingrained habits, steered my decision to return to India.

Financially secure with my pension and accrued savings, I had the means to opt for an independent house. However, a modest multi-storey apartment in Noida seemed more fitting for my solitary existence. Before settling into my chosen sanctuary, a sense of duty and nostalgia prompted me to visit my former superior, Ranji.

Chapter 3

Seasons of Stillness

R anji seemed more available than ever. As I recounted my experiences navigating the challenges of retirement—especially the jarring absence of the support system I had grown accustomed to over the decades—he listened intently. Surprisingly, he had never shown such a keen interest in my personal affairs before.

It was a rare moment of openness, a crack in Ranji's usual reserve. One evening, I poured it all out to him, my voice rough with the weight of isolation, the ache of too much empty time. He listened, his sharp eyes steady on me, and then, almost out of the blue, made a proposition—he invited me to move in with him at his Akbar Road bungalow. At first I dismissed it, thinking he was merely extending a polite, hollow gesture of comfort. But Ranji persisted.

Before I could fully process the offer, my belongings from the Academy warehouse had found their way to the former President's bungalow. In the blink of an eye, I had a room there.

The grand old British-era bungalow was a relic of Delhi's colonial past; its high ceilings were adorned with lazy fans that stirred the air and its verandas stretched wide, shaded by ancient neem trees. Thick white walls held the heat at bay, their plaster chipped in places, revealing the passage of time. Where once the bungalow had echoed with the emptiness of a solitary inhabitant, it now resonated with the camaraderie of two seasoned senior citizens.

My room was adorned with my cherished books—history, policy and philosophy stacked in teetering piles—a mirror of a mind still restless, and a few personal effects. Ranji's was in stark contrast—a sanctuary of simplicity, a few trunks with faded treasures, a yoga mat rolled and kept neatly in the corner, a journal in which he penned his thoughts in tight, meticulous script. A small wooden box sat by his bed, home to prayer beads and a tiny brass bell for his yogic kriyas, the only echoes of a life once lived under the nation's gaze. There was also an old chessboard with worn-out pieces and a pile of yellowing chess journals. His space reflected the man—stripped to his essence—while I clung to the clutter of my yesteryears.

Two men divided by a gap of about fifteen years

and starkly different backgrounds began a new chapter together. Our divergent lineages, appearances, worldviews, tastes and idiosyncrasies provided a contrasting backdrop, yet we found harmony in our coexistence.

Our days soon wove into a rhythm, a gentle cadence of solitude and subtle ties. Ranji rose with the dawn, his lean frame flowing through yoga poses on the veranda, the soft chants of his sadhana blending with the rustle of leaves and the distant calls of mynahs. He tended the garden next, coaxing life from the soil—roses, jasmine and a patch of tulsi thriving under his care—before retreating to his room. I eased into the morning later, tea in hand, the day unfurling as I read or scratched notes on ageing paper.

Breakfast rarely aligned—him with his herbal brew, me with toast and a smear of jam—but lunch became our ritual. We would sit across the long teak dining table, its surface scarred with the ghosts of past feasts, him eating sparingly, me savouring curry or a hunk of bread, the clink of plates a quiet bridge between our worlds. Dinner seldom synced, my late nights clashing with his early fade, but those midday meals spun a thread of constancy through our separate lives.

I slipped into the role of an informal manager, ensuring the household staff were efficient and available. They kept the bungalow humming, a small crew who had become part of its fabric. There was Mohan, the cook—a wiry man with a mop of greying hair and a perpetual grin—who would shuffle in at dawn to knead dough for parathas or simmer a pot of dal, his chatter filling the kitchen with life.

'Sahib, you must try this today,' he would say, sliding a plate my way, his voice bright with pride. 'Too much spice for Ranji Sahib, but just right for you.'

Then there was Kamla, the housekeeper, a stout woman with a no-nonsense air, her sari rustling as she swept the floors and dusted the heavy curtains, muttering about Delhi's dust. She would eye Ranji's sparse room with a frown: 'So little to clean here; he makes my job too easy,' she would grumble, though her tone held a grudging fondness.

Akram, the gardener, was a lanky youth who trailed Ranji in the mornings, learning the names of plants and the art of pruning, his quiet 'Ji Sahib' a constant refrain.

Old Baldev, the driver, sat most days polishing the ancient Ambassador—its cream paint chipped but gleaming, though Ranji rarely asked to be driven anywhere.

The staff hovered more for me than for him, his self-sufficiency a relic of presidential discipline. He cleaned his own room, washed his clothes, fasted often.

At first, I held to my old haunts, escaping to the Gymkhana Club in the evenings, a stately sprawl off Safdarjung Road where Delhi's retired elite gathered. Its lawns rolled green and manicured, dotted with white wicker chairs into which I would sink with a book and a sweating glass of chilled beer. The clubhouse smelled of polished wood and nostalgia, its walls lined with sepia photos of polo matches and viceregal dinners, the chatter of old colleagues a balm against the quiet of home.

'Still reading those dry tomes, are you?' my friend Prakash, a former IAS officer, would tease, his glass clinking against mine.

Some mornings I headed to the Delhi Golf Club, its fairways stretching amid Lodhi-era tombs, peacocks strutting across the greens as I swung at balls with a satisfying thwack, the crisp air sharp with dew. Ranji stayed rooted—his world the bungalow and its garden, his needs few—while I sought the call of company beyond our walls.

But slowly, I drifted inward, drawn to his ways. I would linger in the garden at dusk, watering the plants he had nurtured. Their names—gulmohar, champa, neem—rolled off my tongue from his patient lessons.

'You are getting the hang of it,' he said one evening, his voice low as he handed me a trowel, a rare smile tugging at his lips.

I began cooking frugal meals—dal and rice and a boiled egg—the act soothing in its simplicity.

'Not bad,' Mohan would nod, peering over my shoulder, 'but it needs more cumin.'

Yoga crept into my mornings, my creaking joints

protesting as I mirrored poses I had watched Ranji perfect, his soft 'Breathe, just breathe' guiding me through. Our lives, once distinct, began to overlap, the edges blurring with each season that passed.

Five years unfolded like this, a gentle parade of Delhi's seasons binding us closer. Summers draped the bungalow in a heavy heat, the fans whirring ceaselessly, the garden wilting until Ranji and Akram revived it with buckets of water. 'Too hot for the roses,' Ranji would murmur, wiping his brow, and I would nod, fetching him a glass of water from the kitchen.

Monsoons followed, the veranda slick with rain, the air thick with the scent of wet earth as Kamla grumbled about muddy footprints. 'This city drowns every year,' she would say, wringing out a cloth, while Ranji and I sat watching the downpour in a rare shared silence.

Autumn brought crispness, the neem trees shedding leaves that Baldev swept into piles, the sky a clear blue over the golf course where I still ventured some days. Winters wrapped us in fog, the garden silvered with frost, Mohan brewing extra tea as we huddled by the fire.

We rarely spoke of the past directly, but it lived in the air. I had been his secretary in his presidential years—a younger man threading the corridors of power while he guided the nation with quiet resolve. Now, I helped in smaller ways—drafting speeches for the rare events he attended, piecing together his memoirs from tales he shared over lunch, arranging occasional trips.

'You still write better than I speak,' he would say with a chuckle, reading my drafts, his eyes crinkling at the corners. His voice softened here, tracing a boyhood in a distant hamlet, a swift rise in politics, and I could capture it, preserving a legacy he seemed content to let drift. Our differences—age, lineage and outlook—faded, overtaken by the bond of two men ageing side by side.

The staff noticed it too. 'You are turning into him,' Kamla remarked one day, watching me sweep my room, her hands on her hips. 'Less work for me, I suppose.' Mohan teased, 'Next you will be fasting too, Sahib,' as I skipped a meal, lost in a book. Akram grew bolder, inviting me to join them in the garden. 'Ranji Sahib says you are good with the tulsi now.' Baldev, ever quiet, just nodded when I declined a ride. 'Walking is his way too, I see.'

Ranji watched it all with that faint smile, saying little, but once, over lunch, he mused, 'We are not so different, you and I, not any more.'

I laughed. 'Took me long enough,' and the clink of our plates sealed it.

Then one morning, as I returned from the Golf Club—the March air cool against my skin, the fairways still echoing in my mind—I expected the familiar routine of his day: the soft thud of his steps, the rustle of his mat, the steady rhythm of his breath. The house was still, a profound quiet that pressed against my ribs.

I found him in his room, lying on the floor beside his yoga mat, his face a vision of deep, unshakeable calm, as if he had slipped into a meditation too vast to return from. His chest was still, his hands resting gently at his sides, the serenity of him so absolute it held me there, rooted, waiting for someone to speak the words I already felt in the silence.

Chapter 4

The Fire That Would Not Burn

The morning was heavy, the air thick with a stillness that seemed to choke the world. Ranji lay motionless on the floor. I stood over him, my heart pounding, unwilling to accept what I saw. The sole attendant, Mohan, darted off to call for help after I shouted at him to hurry. My hands trembled as I grabbed my phone, dialling friends, hospitals, the President's House, the Prime Minister's Office (PMO)—anyone who might bring a miracle. Time dragged, each minute stretching into forever.

An ambulance rolled up after a few minutes, its siren slicing through the silence. A weary doctor stepped out, his face lined with exhaustion from a long night shift. He knelt beside Ranji, pressed his fingers to his neck, listened with a stethoscope, then looked at me. 'No sign of life,' he said flatly, as if stating the time. He scratched a few illegible lines on a paper, handed me the death summary, and slumped into a corner to rest, his eyes fluttering shut.

I stared at the paper, the words swimming before me. Ranji, dead? It could not be. I called the PMO again, my voice shaking. 'Ranji is gone,' I said.

The reply was curt. 'Keep it under wraps for now and wait for further instructions.'

The PMO took a call to have a quick cremation. As it turned out, the Prime Minister was preparing for a visiting dignitary of great significance in the coming week. In the interest of diplomacy, it was vital to expedite the mourning process and get it over with before the visit. I nodded to no one and hung up.

The day picked up pace after that, a blur of orders and urgency. The PMO wanted the funeral done quickly—wrapped up before it could disrupt the nation's rhythm. By ten in the morning, Doordarshan and All India Radio announced it: 'Former head of state, Ranji, passes away.'

The media scrambled for old photos and forgotten soundbites while the cremation was scheduled for one in the afternoon at Rajghat. His ashes would later be taken south to his home town for a memorial. None of us were in touch with anyone from his village. There was no time to get someone from that remote place in such a hurry. I was it—his only mourner, his stand-in kin.

An army truck arrived, its engine growling. Soldiers stepped out with the tricolour and wrapped Ranji's body with care. A retreat band played soft, mournful notes as they lifted him on to a pedestal in an open lorry. By eleven, the nation, or at least its leaders, was ready. Priests from every faith gathered, their voices mingling in prayer. The Prime Minister and the President laid wreaths of marigolds, their faces tight with duty. Other VIPs followed, offering brisk respects before hurrying to their seats, eager to move on.

The procession to Rajghat was slow, almost dreamlike. The band's music drifted over the crowd—office workers, pedestrians, curious onlookers. Some tossed petals, their hands unsteady. Others shouted 'Ranji lives on!', their voices ragged. It was grief mixed with something else—confusion, perhaps hope.

At Rajghat, a pyre waited; mango wood was stacked high, laced with sandalwood from a nearby forest depot. The scent hung thick in the air—sweet, cloying and heavy. Soldiers placed Ranji's body atop the logs, and the priests began their rituals: chanting, circling, sprinkling water. The tricolour was folded and removed with ceremony. Then someone handed me a torch. It was my job to light the pyre.

I circled the pyre, the torch's flame flickering. The priests' voices rose, steady and solemn. I paused, drew a breath and thrust the burning stick into the wood. Nothing happened. The timber smoked, thin grey tendrils curling upwards, but no flame. Faces around me hardened with worry, impatience, frustration.

'More wood!' someone shouted. Soldiers rushed to gather dry branches and camphor. Another threw brittle leaves on to Ranji's body.

A fireman stepped forward, his voice low. 'Kerosene would do it,' he murmured.

The head priest glared. 'No,' he snapped. 'This is sacred.'

We waited, the air growing tense. Smoke thickened, stinging my eyes, but still no fire. The priests chanted louder, as if their words could summon flame. The VIPs shifted, muttering among themselves. 'What is taking so long?' the Prime Minister whispered, his voice cutting through the haze. The President frowned but stayed silent.

Hours passed—or maybe minutes; time felt slippery.

And then, just as hope began to fade, faint wisps of smoke began curling higher, darker now, more insistent. A tongue of flame licked the air. Everyone's gaze fixed on the pyre's gradual ignition. In that charged hush, an event so astonishing, so disarming, unfolded that it left all present dumbstruck.

Chapter 5

The Ghost Who Walked

Through the rising smoke and haze, a figure began to stir. It was Ranji, seemingly awakening from a deep trance, unscathed and very much alive. Standing erect, he looked around, confusion evident in his eyes, clearly disoriented by the unexpected backdrop. The chants ceased instantly, replaced by gasps of disbelief from the priests and the onlookers. Around him, the air crackled with confusion. The priests, their chants cut short, stared with wide eyes, clutching their prayer beads as if they could ward off the impossible. Soldiers stood rigid, hands twitching near their rifles, caught between duty and awe. Street vendors, the bangle sellers who had paused their trade to watch, dropped their baskets, letting the doughy rings tumble into the dirt. A cluster of VIPs, dressed in starched kurtas and pristine saris, muttered among themselves.

I was there too, just a few steps away, my heart hammering against my chest. I could not make sense of it. Ranji was alive. Here he was, stepping out of the smoke like a man reborn, or perhaps something else entirely. He did not look at me, did not look at anyone. His face was a blank mask, his first steps shaky, like a newborn calf finding its feet. Then, without a sound, he started walking.

'Where is he going?' a voice shouted from the crowd. I had no answer. Ranji pushed through the swirling smoke, his long strides carrying him forward with a purpose I could not fathom.

I followed, my sandals slapping the ground, my breath catching as I tried to keep pace. He did not glance back, did not acknowledge the chaos erupting behind him. The priests called out blessings, their voices trembling. The soldiers gave orders, their shouts lost in the din. The VIPs scrambled to their cars, engines roaring to life. But Ranji kept moving, and soon he was out of Rajghat, stepping on to the main road where the world exploded into a riot of sound and motion. I, still reeling from shock but driven by an innate sense of duty, quickly followed him, ready to assist and protect him from the bewilderment that awaited.

Hundreds of people were already there, drawn by whispers that had spread faster than the wind: the former President's pyre did not take him. He is alive. Thousands more joined as we walked, a swelling tide of humanity pressing in from all sides. Rickshaws honked, scooters wove through the throng, and street dogs darted between legs, yapping at the commotion. The press descended like vultures, microphones thrust forward, cameras flashing in a blinding storm. 'Sir! Sir! What happened? Where are you going?' they yelled. Ranji did not respond. He did not even turn his head. He walked fast, almost running, his shoulders hunched, his gaze fixed on some unseen point ahead. He moved like a ghost, like a man fleeing a shadow only he could see.

I stayed close, my lungs burning from the effort. 'Ranji,' I said softly, testing his name. He did not react. I was not sure he even heard me. His path veered into the narrow by-lanes around the Red Fort and Chandni Chowk, a labyrinth of history and life that seemed to pull us in. The crowd thinned as the streets tightened, but they did not stop following. Their voices bounced off the ancient stone walls—some praying, some amused, some simply marvelling at the sight of him.

He stopped first at a Jain temple, its white marble façade gleaming in the morning light. Sri Digambar Jain Lal Mandir, built in 1656 during the reign of Mughal emperor Shah Jahan, stood as a quiet testament to peace. Its red sandstone arches and intricate carvings spoke of a time when Jain merchants thrived in the shadow of the Red Fort. Ranji stepped inside, his bare feet silent on the cool floor. The priests froze, their hands mid-gesture, as he bowed his head briefly before moving on. Next came a Hindu temple, the Gauri Shankar Mandir, its roots stretching back to the eighteenth century. Legend said it was built by a Maratha soldier who had prayed to Lord Shiva for victory. Its bells clanged as devotees pressed their palms together, staring at Ranji in awe. He did not linger.

Ranji then walked to the Jama Masjid, its massive domes and minarets towering over the street. Built by Shah Jahan between 1644 and 1656, it was a marvel of Mughal architecture, its courtyard vast enough to hold 25,000 worshippers. The red sandstone glowed warm in the sun, its white marble stripes cutting sharp lines against the sky. Ranji climbed the steps, paused at the arched entrance. At Gurdwara Sis Ganj Sahib, he stood still for a moment, listening to the soft sound of prayers. This sacred site marked the martyrdom of Guru Tegh Bahadur, beheaded in 1675 by Emperor Aurangzeb for defending religious freedom. The golden dome shimmered faintly, a beacon of resilience. Ranji moved on, crossing the road to St Mary's Church, a modest structure built by the British in the nineteenth century. Its wooden doors creaked as he pushed them open, the faint scent of incense drifting out. He did not stay long, walking towards Fatehpuri Mosque with its single dome and quiet courtyard—a gift from Fatehpuri Begum, one of Shah Jahan's queens, built in 1650.

I watched him, my mind spinning. What was he

doing? It was as if he was stitching together a tapestry of faith, threading his way through every place of worship to challenge the idea that religions were at war. Each place he visited bore testimony to his quiet challenge against the narrative of religious strife, his journey a symbol of unity in diversity. Chandni Chowk unfurled before us, a living archive of India's soul. Once called Shahjahanabad, it was laid out in 1650 by Shah Jahan's daughter Jahanara, a boulevard of commerce and culture. Hindus, Muslims, Christians, Sikhs, Jains— they all lived here, their homes and shops pressed tight under the looming Red Fort. This was Delhi's beating heart, a place that had seen Mughal emperors, British colonizers, and countless rulers before them. It had endured invasions, rebellions and the bloody scars of Partition, yet it refused to crumble.

Chandni Chowk, the heart of Old Delhi, was also a testament to time. With every step, stories of poets and warriors, merchants and royalty echoed. There stood the elegant havelis of shayars, adjacent to those of physicians—the vaids, hakims and maulvis...

The air was thick with the scent of ittar—floral perfumes sold in tiny glass vials—and rose milk, its sweetness mingling with the smoky tang of parathas frying in Parathewali Gali. This narrow lane, famous since the 1870s, was a paradise of stuffed flatbreads. Vendors flipped parathas stuffed with potatoes, cauliflower, lentils, even bananas, bubbling with ghee.

'Try one, bhaiya!' a shopkeeper called to me as we passed, holding out a steaming plate. I shook my head, too focused on Ranji to stop. Nearby, kebabs sizzled on open coals, their spiced aroma curling through the streets. Jalebis twisted in hot oil, the golden loops dripping with syrup, while chaat stalls offered tangy golgappas and crispy papdi. Havelis lined the lanes, their carved balconies sagging with age. Once homes to wealthy merchants and poets, these grand houses whispered of a time when shayars like Mirza Ghalib sipped sharbat and spun verses under their roofs.

Ranji moved through it all like he had walked these paths in another life. He did not speak, did not pause to eat or drink. He just kept going, his pace relentless. I trailed him, my legs aching, my mouth dry. 'Excellency, slow down,' I said once, reaching for his arm. He did not pull away, but he did not stop either. His skin was cold, even in the midday heat.

The crowd behind us grew louder, a chorus of believers and doubters. 'He is a saint!' someone cried. 'He has lost his mind!' another snapped. I waved them back, my voice raw. 'Give him space! Let him breathe!' But they did not listen. They pressed closer, hands outstretched, voices begging for answers.

I became his shield, shoving people aside, shouting at the press to back off. When the sky darkened and a soft drizzle began to patter down, I grabbed an umbrella from a vendor and held it over his head. He did not seem to notice.

We passed Gautam Buddha Road, where the air hung heavy with cheap perfume and laughter spilling out from behind shuttered windows. G.B. Road was an oasis of love without judgement. Musicians, irrespective of background, played tunes of unity. No one here cared about faith or caste. Love was their currency, and it crossed all lines. Further on, an old man strummed a sitar in a corner, his fingers weaving melodies that belonged to no religion, only to the heart. A group of wrestlers tumbled out of an akhada, their muscled bodies slick with sweat as they slapped each other's backs. Hindus, Muslims, Sikhs—they trained together, ate together, celebrated Diwali, Eid and Christmas with equal fervour.

Chandni Chowk was India distilled, a place where history and survival intertwined. It had seen Nadir Shah's massacre in 1739, when blood ran through these streets, and the 1857 mutiny against the British, when cannons roared from the Red Fort. It had weathered the Partition riots of 1947 and the anti-Sikh violence of 1984, yet it stood firm, its spirit unbroken. Afghani dry fruits sat in burlap sacks next to Himachali apples and Lucknowi mangoes. A man hawked Bihari litchi, his voice rising over the chatter, while another sold south Indian spices, their sharp scents cutting through the air. In one corner, a barber shaved a man's face with a straight razor while an ear-cleaner worked nearby with a thin metal rod. A tooth-puller yanked out a molar from a wincing customer's mouth—no anaesthesia, just a quick tug and a groan. Life here was raw, unpolished, and Ranji seemed to absorb it all without a word.

Ranji moved effortlessly through this maze, displaying an intimate familiarity with every nook and cranny. The enigmatic aura he carried remained undisturbed. He neither spoke nor acknowledged anyone, seemingly lost in his own world. He was an ethereal entity, a spectral figure making his way through a living orchestra of business and mystique.

He turned into a side lane, his steps sure despite the chaos. I stumbled after him, nearly tripping over a stray cat. 'Where are you going?' I asked loudly. He did not answer. He stopped only once, when we reached the bird market near Fatehpuri Mosque. The narrow street was a cacophony of cages. Parrots squawked, pigeons cooed and sparrows fluttered against their bars. Ranji walked to the nearest stall, reached out, and unlatched a cage. The birds inside hesitated, then broke free, wings beating the air as they soared upwards. The shopkeeper gaped, but Ranji did not pause. He moved to the next cage, then the next, his hands steady as he released them.

The crowd caught the spark. A boy with a gap-toothed grin darted forward and opened another cage. Then another. Soon, people were laughing, shouting, tearing open every cage they could reach. Birds filled the sky, a whirlwind of feathers and freedom. Rabbits hopped between feet, lizards skittered up walls, puppies yipped as they bolted down the street. Even the shopkeepers joined in, their protests melting into grins as they watched the animals scatter. I stood frozen, my heart pounding, as the madness spread. Someone opened a coop of chickens; another freed a flock of goats. A calf bumped against my legs, bleating, before darting off. The air rang with the sound of life breaking loose, a wild, joyous chaos.

'Excellency, what are you doing?' I asked, my voice swallowed by the noise. He did not look at me. He just kept walking, his face unreadable, his eyes locked on something beyond my sight. I followed, my hands trembling as I tried to keep up.

The world was watching now. News vans clogged the main road, reporters tripping over each other to capture him. 'Former President Ranji walks off his pyre!' the headlines would blare. 'A miracle? A mystery?' They would dig into his life soon—his years leading the nation, his quiet retirement, his early days clawing through politics. They would unearth tales of his childhood, deep in the southern forests, in a village so remote it barely existed on maps. They would demand to know why he was here, why he was walking, why he would not speak.

I had no answers to those questions. All I knew was

that I could not abandon him. I became his shadow, his keeper, his voice when he had none. When he sat down on a kerb, exhausted, I spread a small mat beneath him. When he slept, curled up in an alley, I draped a blanket over his shoulders. I forced water past his lips when his face grew pale, coaxed bits of roti into his mouth when he started to shake. I shooed away the crowds, barked at the press, guided the security teams trailing us like lost pets. Once, when he slipped into a shadowy corner to relieve himself, I stood guard, my back to him, my glare daring anyone to approach.

Days blurred into weeks and I lost count. Ranji walked, and I followed. He moved through Delhi like a ghost with a purpose, his silence louder than any speech. The city shifted around him. People stopped to stare, then joined us, their footsteps a steady drumbeat on the stones. Animals trailed in his wake, freed from cages and pens, a strange parade of the living. The central secretariat was busy creating a draft to explain this unprecedented development, scouring back files for any possible precedent. The PMO was contemplating a statement after being doubly sure of the nation's mood. The press grew ravenous, the world more curious. 'Who is he now?' they asked. 'What does he want?'

I did not know.

But I stayed with him, my own life dissolving into his shadow. He was a dead man walking, a soul unbound, and I was the one anchoring him to the earth. One night, as he slept under a flickering streetlamp, I sat beside him, my knees drawn up, my hands pressed to my face. 'Excellency,' I whispered, so softly I barely heard myself. 'What are you searching for?'

He did not move. The wind carried the sounds of distant traffic, the rustle of leaves, the faint cry of a bird he had set free. I leaned back against the wall, my eyes heavy, and wondered how long I could keep chasing a ghost.

Before anyone realized, Ranji had already embarked on his journey, leading us deep into the heart of India— into the raw, uncharted territories where few dared to go.

Chapter 6

The Jungle That Raised Him

Who was Ranji and where did he come from? His roots were indeed fascinating, and perhaps this was what shaped the enigma he became. Born amidst the mesmerizing beauty of a hunter-gatherer terrain, he carried the legacy of his elusive father, Muthu. The legacy was not only of blood, but of whispered tales of valour and mystery that surrounded Muthu's life.

Ranji was not always Ranji. He came into the world nameless, a half-orphan born in a tiny tribal settlement deep within the Kurangani Reserve Forest of Theni, back when it was still a rugged corner of Madurai district. This was not a place one would find on any map. It was a hidden speck, swallowed by the wild expanse of the Western Ghats. The forest spread out like an endless sea of green, its hills rolling in gentle waves, cloaked in trees and mist. This was an elephant corridor—a sacred artery where the giants of the jungle roamed freely, their paths carved through centuries of instinct.

For the people here, civilization was a distant rumour. Their only ties to the outside world were the tea and spice estates that crept up the slopes like stubborn weeds, and the poachers who slunk through the shadows with eyes glinting with greed for ivory.

Kurangani was a living, breathing thing, alive with secrets and stories. Teak trees towered above, their trunks thick and straight, their broad leaves whispering in the wind that swept down from the peaks. Shola forests crowned the higher ridges, gnarled and moss-covered, fog-drenched at dawn and dusk. Wild pepper vines snaked around the tree trunks, their tiny green fruits pungent and sharp, the scent mingling with the earthy sweetness of cardamom bushes tucked in the shadows. Coffee plants peppered the undergrowth, their red berries glowing like drops of blood. Flame-of-the-forest trees erupted in brilliant orange, the petals falling to the ground like embers. Orchids clung to branches, fragile and wild, their colours purple, white, yellow, flashing in the filtered sunlight. Bamboo groves stood in clusters, their hollow stalks creaking and groaning as the breeze pushed through; the forest floor was a carpet of ferns, wild grasses and fallen leaves—soft but treacherous with hidden roots and thorns.

Life pulsed in every corner. Elephants rumbled

through the trails, their massive feet thudding against the earth, their trumpets reverberating across the hills like thunder. Herds of gaur, the hulking Indian bison, grazed in open patches, their dark, glossy hides rippling with muscle. Sambar deer darted through the trees, escaping danger, their antlers snagging on vines. Leopards stalked silently, their golden eyes glowing in the shadows, their spotted coats blending with the dappled light. Sloth bears foraged with grunts, snouts buried in termite mounds. High above, Nilgiri langurs swung through the canopy, their black faces peering down as their hoots echoed. Hornbills glided with a heavy beat of wings; kingfishers streaked past in flashes of blue and orange. Peacocks strutted in clearings, their iridescent tails fanning out in dazzling arcs, while parakeets screeched in flocks, their green feathers blending with the leaves. On the ground, cobras slithered through grasses, their hoods flaring; monitor lizards basked on warm rocks, their tongues flicking lazily. Butterflies danced in the air like shards of stained glass, while bees buzzed around wildflowers, their hum a constant drone in the forest's chorus.

This was the world where Ranji's story took root, a place of raw beauty and quiet danger, where his father, Muthu, became a legend whispered around fires.

Muthu was a small man, wiry and tough, with skin like the bark of a teak tree—dark, rough, and weathered by the sun and rain. His hair fell past his shoulders in thick, matted clumps, the wild tangle streaked with dust and leaves. His eyes, sharp and restless, glinted with a wildness that set him apart, as if he were always listening to something no one else could hear. He wore a faded lungi, the cloth stained with mud and tied tight around a narrow waist; his feet were cracked and broad, hardened by years of running barefoot through the jungle. His face was all edges: a crooked nose from some long-ago fight, a scar down his left cheek—jagged and white against his skin. Perhaps it came from a thorn, perhaps a claw, no one knew, and Muthu never said. He did not smile much, his mouth a thin, silent line, but when he moved, it was with the quick, graceful alertness of a deer.

His wife, Selvi, was his opposite in every way. Small and frail, her body bent from a lifetime of struggle, she walked with a limp from a twisted leg she'd carried since birth. Blind from the day she was born, her eyes were clouded, like the mist that hung over the hills at dawn, and they never quite focused on anything. Her hair, thin and greying, was always pulled into a knot that unravelled by midday, and her skin was dark and creased, etched with lines from the sun and the wind. She wore a cotton sari, patched and faded, its edges frayed and dragging through the dirt as she worked. Her hands were gentle, always fumbling as she felt her way through life, but they were strong too—picking tea leaves or steadying sticks with quiet determination.

Selvi's voice was soft, almost lost in the forest's noise, but it had a warmth that made people listen. She hummed old tribal songs while sorting leaves in the tea gardens, her fingers moving by memory alone, and when she laughed, it was a rare, bright sound, like a bird breaking into song.

The tribe told stories about Muthu's early years, how he had vanished into the forest as a boy, chasing a butterfly, a big one with yellow wings. For years, they thought him dead, swallowed by the jungle. But then he returned years later—older, naked and howling. His body was lean and scarred, hair matted, teeth bared. The elders swore he had been raised by elephants—that he had slept in their shade, eaten berries from their trunks, learnt their language. He tore off any clothes given to him, ran wild and spoke only in grunts and shrieks. It took months to tame him, to teach him to wear a lungi, to sit still by the fire, to eat with his hands.

Selvi had been an outcast until Muthu came along. The tribe pitied her—a blind girl with a twisted leg who had no hope of a husband or a future. But Muthu saw something in her. One evening, as the sun sank behind the hills, he stood before the elders with Selvi beside him. His words were clumsy as he tried to convey his proposal. 'I will stay with her.'

The elders frowned, their brows creased with doubt, but Muthu did not waver. Selvi giggled, her hands twisting the edge of her sari. '*Ava kadu satham enaku kaathula vizhum',* she said, 'His jungle sounds seem sweet to my ears.'

They were married beneath a banyan tree, the tribe gathered round, women singing and men beating drums made of stretched hides. Muthu became Selvi's eyes, guiding her through the forest with his hands on her shoulders, describing the world in his broken way. *'Pacha ilai, periya maram',* he'd mutter, 'green leaves, big tree.'

She gave him her words, teaching him Tamil bit by bit, softening his wild cries into something human. *'Enna paaru,'* she would say, 'look at me', and he would try. They were two halves of a whole, mending each other's cracks.

Muthu and Selvi lived in a mud hut at the edge of the settlement—a structure of packed earth and straw, its roof thatched with palm fronds that rustled in the wind. Inside, it was sparse. A woven mat on the floor, a clay pot for water and a small fire pit that filled the air with smoke. A few chipped bowls sat in a corner, and a bundle of dried herbs hung from the ceiling, their sharp scent cutting through the damp. They did not have much, but they did not need much. They had each other, and that was enough.

Life was hard, but they carved out a quiet happiness. Selvi worked in the tea gardens, her fingers sorting leaves by touch, while Muthu roamed the forest, gathering firewood or hunting small game—rabbits, wild chickens, sometimes a fish from the stream. At night, they would sit by their fire, Selvi humming, Muthu tapping his foot to the rhythm. *'Nalla paatu,'* he would say, 'good song,' his voice still rough but softer now. She would smile and lean against him, her head on his shoulder, the firelight dancing on her face. For a while, it seemed the forest would let them be. But peace never lasted long in Kurangani.

Those were the days of the ivory trade, a dark shadow that crept over the hills. Poachers flooded the forest, their boots trampling the trails, their guns glinting in the sun. They hunted elephants for their tusks—long, milky teeth that fetched gold in far-off lands. Ivory was carved into bangles, statues, bowls and trinkets, shipped to Europe, America, anywhere people had money to flaunt. Thousands of elephants fell, their bodies left to rot as their tusks sailed across the seas. In Kurangani, the herds dwindled, retreating deeper into the forest, their calls growing faint. The poachers grew desperate, and then they heard about Muthu, the boy who had lived with elephants, who could summon them with a cry.

It started as whispers in the tea gardens. 'Muthu knows the herd,' the workers said. 'He talks to them.' One night, as the moon hung low, a gang of poachers stormed the settlement. They dragged Muthu from his hut, their hands rough, their voices sharp.

Selvi screamed, clawing at the air. *'Vidu! Naan*

thanniya irukkaa! Let him go! I am here alone!' she cried, her voice cracking.

Muthu thrashed about, his wildness flaring, but they were too many. They hauled him to their camp, a filthy sprawl of tents in a clearing, stinking of sweat, liquor, tobacco and gunpowder. Lanterns flickered, casting long shadows, and the air buzzed with mosquitoes. They shoved him into a rickety shed and locked the tin door.

'Call the elephants!' they barked, their fists slamming into his ribs. Muthu's body was tough, forged by the jungle, and he did not flinch. He stared at them, his eyes burning, his lips sealed.

Days passed. The beatings worsened. They shouted, lashed him with sticks, even burned his arm with hot iron. He endured it all, his face blank, his body unyielding. Then they turned crueller. They dragged him back to the village and hauled out his father, Perumal, and uncle, Chinnan, from their huts. Selvi stumbled after, her hands outstretched, her voice raw. *'Enna pannureenga? Ava kozhandhaiya vittudu!* What are you doing? Leave the child alone!' she begged, clutching her swollen belly.

The poachers did not care. They shot Perumal and Chinnan in front of the tribe. Blood soaked the soil, their bodies crumpling like sacks. Selvi collapsed, wailing, while Muthu roared, a sound more animal than human.

They took him again, along with Kannan, a skinny

boy who cooked their meals, his hands trembling as he stirred pots. The poachers locked Muthu in the shed again. 'Call them now, or your wife is next,' they snarled. Muthu sat there on the floor, dirt streaking his face, tears cutting tracks, his hands shaking. '*En appa, en chithappa*,' he whispered, 'My father, my uncle,' over and over, a broken chant. The poachers leaned in, gun ready, waiting.

Then Muthu did something no one could have foreseen.

He threw back his head and let out a sound—a deep rumbling howl that shook the trees, rolling through the Kurangani forest, loud and wild, followed by sharp piercing shrieks no ordinary throat could make. The poachers froze, their grins spreading, thinking their prize was near.

The forest fell silent, the birds hushed, the wind stalled. In the distance, a lone female elephant stepped into the clearing, her trunk swaying, her ears flapping gently. Her eyes gleamed with a knowing calm, as if she had heard Muthu's call across lifetimes.

The poachers raised their guns, expecting a herd to follow, their greed blinding them to the tremor beneath their feet. The ground began to shake. A low rumble grew into a thunderous roar. From every corner of the forest elephants came charging—not hundreds, but enough to fill the clearing with their fury. Their massive bodies crashed through the trees, trunks blaring, feet pounding, eyes blazing with rage. The camp was a fragile speck against their might. Tents crumpled like dry leaves, guns snapped like twigs, and the poachers' screams were swallowed by the chaos. Pots and pans flew, landing in the bushes. Bullets scattered uselessly, lost in the storm of dust and wrath. Amid the turmoil, only Kannan, who had slipped Muthu extra rice and spoken to him with kindness, was spared. He crouched behind a fallen log, his heart pounding, his eyes wide with terror and awe.

When the dust settled the camp was a ruin. The poachers were gone, some crushed, others having fled into the night. The elephants stood still, their breathing heavy, their presence a wall of unyielding strength. But Muthu was nowhere to be found.

The big bull elephant, its tusks chipped and grey, stood at the clearing's edge, its trunk raised as if in farewell. Had it carried Muthu away, lifting him on to its back like a king on a throne? Or had the poachers, in their final act of vengeance, taken him before the herd arrived? Some whispered of an old shed crumbled under the stampede's force, its timbers hiding a body never found. Others swore they saw Muthu vanish into the jungle's heart, his form blending with the shadows, perhaps choosing the elephants' path over a world that had broken his heart. The truth remained a mystery, a wound that bled with questions no one could answer.

Kannan stumbled back to the village, his legs weak,

his voice trembling as he told the tale. '*Muthu avana kadu raja madhiri poitaaru,*' he said, 'He left like a jungle king.' His voice was choked with tears, his hands shaking as he described the elephants' fury and Muthu's haunting cry. The villagers gathered around, their faces etched with grief and wonder, their whispers weaving a story that grew with each telling. Was Muthu dead, his body lost to the poachers' cruelty or the forest's embrace? Had he joined the elephants, becoming one with the wild that had raised him? Or had he slipped away, a ghost fleeing the pain of a life torn apart? The mystery clung to the air, heavy as the mist that draped the hills at dawn.

Selvi was alone now, her heart shattered, her belly round with their child. She worked the tea gardens until her legs buckled, her blind hands sorting leaves by feel, each motion a quiet act of survival. '*En purushan enna vittutu poitaaru, aana avan kozhandhai enaku irukku,*' she would whisper, 'my husband left me, but his child is with me.' Her voice trembled with love and loss, her cloudy eyes wet with tears. The women of the tribe watched over her, their hands gentle as they brought her rice and tapioca, their voices soft as they rubbed her back when the pains came. They shared her grief, their own hearts heavy with the mystery of Muthu's fate, yet they held her close, a family forged by the jungle's trials.

One evening, under a banyan tree with roots sprawling like ancient fingers, Selvi went into labour.

The women gathered around, their voices a soft murmur, their hands steady as they guided her through the agony. She screamed, her cries echoing through the forest, her frail body shaking with the effort. Sweat beaded her brow, her blind eyes searching for a husband who was no longer there. *'Muthu, enna paaru,'* she gasped, 'look at me,' as if he might hear her across the void. The women held her hands, their tears mingling with hers, their strength carrying her through the pain. At last, a boy slipped into the world, small and crying, his tiny voice a spark of life in the gathering dusk. They named him nothing at first, simply 'Muthu's son,' a fragile link to the man who had vanished.

Selvi held her child close, her cloudy eyes glistening, her fingers tracing his face as she had once traced Muthu's. She smiled, a fleeting moment of joy amidst her sorrow, and then her breath faded, her body still as the last light left her. The women wept, their hands cradling the newborn as they mourned the mother who had given him life. The tribe took the boy in, feeding him goat's milk, singing him the songs of a father who might be a king, a ghost, or a memory lost to the jungle. The Kurangani forest cradled him, its trees and rivers and beasts shaping him as they had shaped Muthu. He would grow up wild and silent, his eyes carrying his father's glint, his steps echoing a mystery that would never be solved, a boy born of love and loss, destined to wander under the shadow of his father's unanswered fate.

Chapter 7

The Boy with a Hundred Names

The Kurangani forest mourned in silence, its trees whispering secrets of loss. The village, bound by shared grief, came together as one family to cradle a child left alone by fate. Ranji was not merely an orphan; he was the son of the entire hamlet, cherished and nurtured by a plethora of sisters, grannies and distant uncles who poured their love into his small, quiet world. Life in the hamlet was simple, woven with warmth, stories and the soft zest for survival. Yet beneath the surface lay a tender ache, the memory of Muthu's mysterious disappearance and Selvi's fleeting life, their absence a shadow that clung to the boy's every step.

Whenever a visitor of importance—a government officer, a curious traveller or a politician seeking votes— arrived in the hamlet, little Ranji was presented like a precious gem. It was a Tamil tradition, a way to honour the guest by letting them name a child. The sight of a boy with no parents stirred hearts, and in return the visitors offered aseervadam, blessings for a good life, along with small gifts—a few rupees, a sweet or a gentle pat. Each name they gave carried a piece of their hopes or whims. 'Punmudi', one called him, meaning golden hair, inspired by the sunlight catching his curls. Another named him 'Shivaji', dreaming of a warrior's strength, while a third chose 'Naikar', meaning leader, sensing a spark in his quiet eyes. The grandmothers had their own names, soft and woven with affection—Little Sparrow for his quick movements, Son of the Wind for his love of running through the forest... Before he had one true name, Ranji carried hundreds, each a thread in the village's love for him.

The women who raised him told stories under the banyan tree, their voices thick with emotion. *'Un appa oru kadu raja',* they would say, 'your father was a jungle king', recounting Muthu's wild call and the elephants' charge, their eyes misty with pride and sorrow. Ranji listened, his small face solemn, his heart heavy with tales of a father he could not remember and a mother whose touch he could not recall. He clung to these tales, letting them shape his dreams. He spoke little, his thoughts hidden behind a gaze that seemed to see beyond the trees.

Everything changed when Father Thomas arrived

from a distant district. A gentle man with a soft voice and a fiery wish to propagate his faith, he came with helpers to build a church in the habitation. The air soon carried hymns every Sunday, their melodies drifting over the forest like a new kind of birdsong. The villagers gathered for weekly masses, drawn by the promise of free food as much as by curiosity. During one such gathering, Father Thomas looked at Ranji, his eyes kind but resolute.

'This boy needs a name for the world,' he said, his voice carrying over the crowd. He baptized him as Ranjeeth, a name popular among neo-Christians, borrowed from the north. The villagers watched, some nodding, others whispering, as water touched Ranji's forehead. For a moment he was no longer just the hamlet's son; he was a child of a wider world, marked by a new beginning. Yet Ranji, even at five, stood quiet, his eyes fixed on the ground, accepting the name with the same stillness he carried everywhere.

◆

The world beyond Kurangani was shifting, its changes creeping into the forest like unwelcome vines. A global outcry against the ivory trade had declared elephants threatened, and the forest department tightened its grip on poaching. The trade, once a dark tide, grew too risky, pushing lawbreakers to smuggle timber and sandalwood instead. The forest, once a sanctuary, became a hideout for criminals. Kidnappings for ransom, illegal liquor, opium and cannabis trades sprouted like weeds, choking the peace. The forest department doubled its patrols, and police raids swept through the village, searching for wrongdoers. Smugglers, cloaking themselves as modern heroes who stole from the rich, bullied the tribals into silence. Caught in the crossfire, the villagers were trusted by no one. Forest officials saw them as accomplices, while smugglers accused them of betrayal.

Father Thomas, overwhelmed by the chaos, left for safer lands, his dreams of faith crumbling like dry leaves. The church closed its doors, its hymns fading into memory. Without the priest, the tribals returned to their ancient ways, praying to trees, rocks, waterfalls and the spirits of their ancestors. Some began visiting nearby temples, their footsteps soft on sacred ground, while a few ashrams took root near the forest, the chants emanating from the buildings mingling with the wind. Ranjeeth's baptized name slipped away, too formal for the tribal heart. He became Ranji again, a name that felt like the rustle of leaves, like home. *'Ranji, en chellam,'* the grannies would coo, 'my darling,' stroking his hair, their voices thick with love.

At seven, Ranji was sent to a government tribal school ten kilometres away, a boarding school with mud walls and a tin roof. He hated the cold cots and the strange faces, often sneaking back to the hamlet through forest paths he knew by heart. The school's true gift was the noon meal: hot rice, sambar and sometimes a boiled egg, a feast that filled his belly. One teacher, Mr Raman, saw a quiet light in Ranji's eyes.

'You are quick, boy,' he said one day, his voice gruff but kind, as he handed Ranji a tattered book. 'Read this. It is about the world.' Ranji took it, his fingers trembling, and sat under a tamarind tree, sounding out words that opened doors in his mind. Mr Raman taught him to write and count, sparking a curiosity that burned softly, like an ember in the dark. '*Nalla padikkanum, Ranji,*' he would say, 'study well, Ranji,' his hand heavy on the boy's shoulder. Ranji nodded, his lips pressed tight, his heart swelling with a shy pride.

A District Education Officer visited one spring, a stern man with sharp eyes and wearing a crisp shirt. He watched Ranji solve a maths problem on the chalkboard, his answers fast and certain.

'This boy has a gift,' he said, his voice firm, turning to Mr Raman. 'He deserves more than this school can offer.' The teacher's face lit up, but Ranji stood still, his gaze on the floor, unsure of what it meant. The officer's words changed everything. Soon Ranji was enrolled in the Adi Dravidar School in the plains of Periyakulam. They gave him a scholarship, a crisp white shirt and blue shorts and a stack of books. For the first time, Ranji felt the world stretching wide, though his heart ached for the forest's familiar embrace.

The school was a large building of cement and

mortar, with a hostel, a playground and a promise of something bigger. The hostel was a long, low building, with rows of metal cots creaking under restless boys. The shared bathroom smelled of blocked drains, and Ranji missed the open sky. Yet he wore his uniform with quiet pride, its stiffness a badge of his new path. '*Nalla dress, Ranji*,' a hostel mate teased, 'nice clothes, Ranji,' grinning as Ranji smoothed the shirt with careful hands. He nodded, his smile faint, his thoughts elsewhere. After finishing tenth grade, he received a bicycle through a government programme, its wheels granting him freedom to roam the plains. He completed school with strong marks, his teachers' praise a soft glow in his chest, and moved on to an Arts and Science college in Madurai, still supported by his scholarship. The hamlet became a home he carried in his heart.

In the hostel, his roommate was Arul, a wiry boy with a quick laugh and a knack for fixing broken things. 'You are too quiet, Ranji,' Arul said one evening, tossing a cricket ball across their small room. 'Come play. Loosen up!'

Ranji caught the ball, his fingers curling around it, but shook his head. 'Perhaps later,' he murmured, his voice soft, his eyes drifting to the window where the plains stretched wide.

Arul sighed, undeterred. 'You are like a forest spirit, always thinking,' he said, flopping on to the cot.

'But I will get you out there one day.' Ranji's lips

curved slightly, a rare smile, and he returned to his book, the words pulling him into a world of history and rivers.

They spent evenings on the dusty field, Arul batting with gusto while Ranji fielded, his movements quick but silent, his mind half in the game, half in the forest he missed.

The hostel warden, Mr Murugan, watched Ranji like a hawk. A gruff man with a limp from his days as a forest guard, he saw potential in the boy's quiet focus. 'You have a brain, Ranji,' he said one morning, his voice rough as he handed him a map. 'Learn this. It is the forest's secrets.'

Ranji studied the lines, his fingers tracing trails he knew by heart, his eyes bright with recognition. *'Nalla paiyan,'* Mr Murugan muttered, 'good boy,' slapping his shoulder. 'Do not let that mind go to waste.'

Those lessons sank deep, teaching Ranji to read animal tracks, spot healing plants and navigate by stars. They felt more real than the schoolbooks, tying him to the forest even as he walked the plains. Above all, Mr Murugan taught him one more lesson. He played chess with Ranji, a game that had a profound impact on his life and his destiny.

College in Madurai was a new world, alive with the hum of autorickshaws, vendors and stray dogs. Ranji studied history and geography—subjects that sparked when he tied them to the forest's stories.

One evening Ranji and Arul sat by the river, eating cheap vada, the spicy tang burning their tongues.

'I will build bridges,' Arul said, his eyes gleaming.

'Big ones, across rivers like this.' Ranji chewed slowly, his gaze on the water. 'I will work in the forest,' he said softly, his voice barely above a whisper.

Arul laughed, nudging him. 'Always the forest, eh? You are a tree in a man's body.'

Ranji smiled, his heart warm, though he said nothing more, letting the river's flow carry his thoughts.

The forest department had launched the Ecotourism Society to protect the woods and help tribals earn a living. Ranji, still in college, joined them part-time during vacations, drawn by the call of the trees. He started as a helper, carrying bags, cooking meals and guiding trekkers along winding trails. His feet knew every root and rock, his eyes caught every rustle of leaves and his quiet presence calmed even the loudest city folk. The trekkers liked him, charmed by his soft-spoken ways and the forest wisdom he shared without boasting.

One summer evening, he sat with some tribals at the society's camp, the fire crackling under a starry sky. Kala, a wiry woman with a scar on her cheek, nudged him. 'You are good with those city people, Ranji,' she said, her voice warm. 'They listen to you.'

Ranji shrugged, poking the fire with a stick. 'They are not so different,' he said quietly. 'Simply louder, with more money.'

Kala chuckled, her eyes crinkling.

A forest officer, Mr Nair, overheard them, his clipboard tucked under his arm. 'Kala is right,' he said, stepping closer. 'You have a gift, Ranji. You are wasted on carrying bags. Lead a trek next time.'

Ranji's heart raced, but he nodded, his face calm. 'I will try,' he said, his voice steady despite the flutter in his chest.

The next day, he led a small group of four friends, their fancy boots and sunglasses out of place in the wild. Their leader, Vikram, was loud, his questions spilling like a river. 'What is that bird, Ranji?' he asked, spotting a flash of blue.

'Kingfisher,' Ranji answered, his tone soft. 'It likes fish, not people.'

Vikram laughed, slapping his back. 'You are a quiet one, but you know your stuff. Tell us more.'

Ranji led them up a steep trail, pausing at a clearing. 'Those hills,' he said, his voice low, 'my people say spirits live there. They watch us.'

The group gasped, their cameras clicking, their voices bright with wonder. At the trek's end, Vikram pressed some money into Ranji's hand. 'You are the best guide we have ever had,' he said. 'We will be back.'

Ranji accepted the money with a nod, his eyes on the forest, not the coins.

Back at camp another tribal, Suresh, tall and quiet like Ranji, pulled him aside. 'You are making us proud,' he said, his voice earnest. 'Keep going. Maybe they will trust us more.'

Ranji looked at the ground, his fingers twisting a blade of grass. 'I just like the forest,' he said softly.

Suresh smiled, a rare warmth in his eyes. 'That is why you are good,' he said, clapping Ranji's shoulder.

During another trek Mr Nair joined them, watching Ranji guide a group of fifteen through the path. At a waterfall, they swam and ate, their laughter echoing. 'You have talent, Ranji,' Mr Nair said later, his tone firm. 'Stay with us.'

Ranji nodded, his heart full. 'I will, when I am not studying,' he said.

'But do not forget the forest. It is not only a job.'

'I will not,' he promised.

Mr Nair's eyes softened. 'It is in your blood.'

One vacation a storm hit, soaking his group of ten trekkers. 'Ranji, what now?' a man shouted, clutching his hood.

'Follow me,' Ranji called out, and led them to a rock overhang.

They huddled, wet but safe, the rain drumming around them. 'Tell us a story,' a boy begged, his eyes wide.

Ranji hesitated, then grinned faintly. 'Once a tiger chased my uncle,' he said, his voice low. 'He climbed a tree, but the tiger waited three days. Uncle won. He sang until the tiger left.'

Laughter broke the tension, the group's fear easing. When the rain stopped, they hugged him goodbye. 'You are our hero,' the boy's mother said, her voice warm. Ranji ducked his head, his cheeks flushing, and said nothing.

Back at the village Ranji used his earnings to fix leaky roofs and buy seeds for the fields. Arul visited once during a college break. Sprawled on the hostel floor, he said, 'You are still a wanderer.'

'And you are still tall,' Ranji replied, his tone dry. They laughed, the sound filling the small room, a moment of lightness in Ranji's quiet world.

Another forest officer, Mrs Latha, met him at camp one summer. 'You are helping us, Ranji,' she said, her voice kind. 'The tribals need this. Teach them too. Ecotourism will bring more than any other forest work.'

Ranji began showing Kala and Suresh how to read maps, his voice patient as he traced paths with a stick. '*Ithu nalla vazhi*,' he said, 'this is a good path,' his eyes bright with purpose.

Each vacation he grew bolder, suggesting new routes. 'There is a cave on that ridge,' he told Mr Nair, his tone steady. 'Bats live there. People will love it.'

Mr Nair nodded. 'Plan it. You lead.'

The treks grew wilder—peaks with views that stole the breath, groves so thick the sun barely peeked through. Ranji learned to spot trouble: monsoon clouds, a snake's hiss, a twisted ankle—and fix it fast. His backpack held bandages, salt for leeches and a worn-out flute, its notes a soft echo of the forest's song.

Mr Murugan's words stayed with him, a quiet anchor through his college years. Ranji was not only a part-time guide, he was the forest's voice, even with exams looming. The boy with hundreds of names from passing visitors had found his place, one trek at a time. Yet beneath his calm exterior lay a heart that carried the villagers' love, the forest's call, and the unspoken weight of a father's mystery and a mother's fleeting touch. Ranji walked softly, his silence a strength, his steps a promise to the wild that had shaped him.

Chapter 8

The Flames of Fate

A group of college girls from the bustling city of Chennai had ventured into the wilderness to celebrate International Women's Day, their hearts brimming with excitement and their minds free of the shadows that awaited them. For most, it was their first taste of the forest, a world so alien to the concrete jungles they called home.

Ranji, the young man who had carved a life for himself from the ashes of an orphaned childhood, had been appointed their guide by the Ecotourism Committee. Self-taught and resourceful, he carried a quiet strength that belied his humble beginnings. The girls, with their city-bred chatter and untested enthusiasm, took to him instantly. He led them along the winding trails, his voice steady as he pointed out the secrets of the forest: the call of a distant bird, the rustle of a hidden creature and the faint perfume of wildflowers clinging to life amidst the drought.

The dry season had stripped the trees bare, their leaves carpeting the ground in a brittle, golden shroud. The grass, too, had withered under the relentless sun, turning the forest floor into a tinderbox of flammable twigs, leaves and blades that crunched underfoot. The Forest Department, perhaps lulled by the quiet of the season, had neglected to clear the fire lines, leaving behind a silent promise of chaos. The group's destination was a tea garden nestled in the hills, a place of rustic beauty where they planned to camp for the night.

As dusk fell, the campsite came alive with the crackle of a campfire. Ranji, ever the diligent guide, bustled about, helping the girls cook a simple meal of rice and lentils over the open flame. The group had brought bottles of liquor, and soon the air was thick with giggles and the clink of tin cups. A portable speaker blared Tollywood hits that echoed through the stillness of the tea garden, leading the girls into an impromptu dance. They twirled and swayed, their shadows leaping against the flickering light, while Ranji watched from the sidelines, a faint smile tugging at his lips.

One of the girls, a spirited soul named Prema, grabbed his arm and pulled him into the circle. 'Come on, Ranji! Do not be a spoilsport!' she teased, her eyes sparkling with mischief. He relented, his awkward steps drawing cheers and laughter from the group. For a few precious hours, the world was a place of joy, unburdened by the weight of tomorrow.

Liquor flowed freely, and the night stretched on. Stories were shared, tales of college crushes, dreams of the future and the thrill of being far from home.

Amid this fun and frolic sat a quiet girl, Radha— plump, unsure and a little out of place. She had brought a chessboard and was looking for a partner. Ranji had learned the moves from Mr Murugan. He sat with Radha and tried his hand. After a few moves the inevitable happened. He was checkmated.

The fire dwindled to embers, and one by one, the girls retreated to their tents, their voices fading into sleepy murmurs. Ranji stayed awake a little longer, tending to the campsite, ensuring the fire was safely out. The stars above glittered like a promise, and the cool night air wrapped around him like a gentle embrace. He felt a quiet pride in his role, a sense of belonging he had rarely known.

The next morning arrived in a sluggish haze. The girls, bleary-eyed from the revelry, woke up late, their laughter replaced by groans as they nursed mild hangovers. Ranji urged them to pack up, but they moved slowly, reluctant to leave the cocoon of the tea garden. By the time they set out, the sun was already high, its heat pressing down on the parched landscape.

The trek to the hilltop was arduous, the dry grass crunching beneath their feet, the naked trees offering no respite. Sweat beaded their foreheads, and the chatter of the previous night was replaced by tired silence. At last, they reached the summit, where a lone pine tree stood like a sentinel, its branches casting a meagre patch of shade. All around, the hillside stretched out in a sea of brittle yellow, dotted with skeletal trees that seemed to whisper warnings in the wind.

They paused to rest beneath the pine, water bottles being passed around in a quiet ritual. The afternoon sun blazed mercilessly. Ranji scanned the horizon, his instincts prickling with unease. It was then that he saw it—a thin wisp of smoke curling in the distance, a harbinger of the nightmare to come. Within moments, the wisp thickened into a roiling cloud, and the faint crackle of flames reached their ears. The wind, dry and relentless, swept through the valley, fanning the fire into a beast of fury. The girls froze, their eyes wide with disbelief as smoke billowed closer, the air growing heavy with the acrid scent of burning grass.

Panic erupted like a dam breaking. The girls screamed and scattered, their voices swallowed by the rising roar of the fire. Ranji's heart pounded as he shouted over the chaos, his voice raw with desperation. 'Stay calm! Follow me! We can make it out!'

But fear had taken root, and his words were lost in the wind. The flames raced towards them, a wall of orange and red devouring the dry grass with terrifying speed. Naked trees caught like torches, branches snapping and popping. The heat was unbearable, a suffocating force pressing against their skin, stealing the breath from their lungs.

Ranji seized control, his mind racing as he searched for a way out. He spotted a rocky path cutting through the hillside. It was a steep, treacherous descent, but their only hope. 'This way!' he bellowed, waving his arms.

Eleven of the forty girls heeded his call, their faces pale with terror as they stumbled after him. The path was unforgiving, a jagged trail of sharp stones and loose gravel. The girls slipped and fell, their knees and palms scraped raw, their cries mingling with the distant shrieks of those left behind.

Ranji moved among them, urging them forward, his voice a lifeline in the chaos. 'Keep going! Do not stop!' he pleaded, his own hands bloodied from steadying them.

Radha, younger than the rest, struggled under the weight of her backpack, her steps faltering as the slope grew steeper, her round face flushed with exertion. Ranji saw her lagging and rushed to her side. 'Leave the bag, Radha! It's slowing you down!' he urged, his tone gentle but firm.

She shook her head, tears streaming down her cheeks. 'No, it is mine! Everything I have is in here!' she sobbed, clutching the straps as if they were her last tether to safety.

Ranji's heart ached at her innocence, but there was

no time to argue. He pressed on, guiding the others, glancing back to ensure Radha followed.

Then disaster struck. Radha's ankle twisted beneath her; a sharp cry escaped her lips as she crumpled to the ground. The fire was closing in, its heat licking at their heels, the smoke thickening into a choking veil.

Ranji doubled back, his chest tight with dread. 'Get up! We have to move!' he shouted, kneeling beside her. She whimpered, her face contorted in pain, unable to stand. The others had pushed ahead, their figures fading into the haze. Ranji tried to lift her, but her weight and the backpack made it impossible. The fire roared closer, a monstrous wave of heat and light, and Ranji felt a surge of helplessness. 'Please, Radha, let it go!' he begged, his voice breaking.

She nodded at last, her hands trembling as she shed the bag. Ranji tossed it aside, watching the flames swallow it in an instant. He hoisted her on to his back, her arms wrapped around his neck, her sobs muffled against his shoulder.

The fire was upon them now, a deafening symphony of destruction. Ranji staggered forward, the heat searing his skin, the smoke stinging his eyes. He could feel her weight dragging him down, but he refused to falter. Then something extraordinary happened. The flames, so fierce and unstoppable, seemed to part before him. They danced at his feet, then receded, as if held back by an unseen hand.

Ranji stumbled on, disbelief warring with exhaustion, Radha's weight a constant burden. Step by agonizing step, they reached the stony patch beyond the fire's grasp, sliding down the rocky slope until they collapsed at the bottom.

Villagers from a nearby settlement had seen the smoke and rushed to help. They fashioned a makeshift stretcher from branches and cloth, lifting Radha on to it as Ranji caught his breath. The eleven other girls who had followed him emerged from the rocks, their faces streaked with dirt and tears, but alive. They were too shaken to linger, their eyes darting towards the road ahead. A bus rumbled into view, and they clambered aboard, bound for the district headquarters. Ranji watched them go, his chest tight with a mix of relief and dread. He couldn't rest—not yet. The girl he had carried, Radha, lay still, her breathing shallow but steady. Others were still trapped on the hilltop, and he had to find them.

With a handful of villagers, Ranji trekked back up the slope, the fading light casting long shadows across the ravaged landscape. Police, forest officials and a few doctors joined them, their faces grim as they surveyed the devastation. The fire had burned itself out, leaving behind a wasteland of ash and ruin. The air was thick with the stench of charred flesh, a sickening reminder of the lives lost.

As they reached the hilltop, the sight that greeted them was a tableau of horror. Burnt bodies lay scattered across the ground, twisted and blackened beyond recognition. Yet some were still alive, their moans piercing the silence, blistered hands reaching for help.

'Water...please...' one girl rasped, her voice barely a whisper. Ranji knelt beside her, his hands trembling as he offered his bottle. Her eyes fluttered shut before she could drink.

The night that followed the blaze was a cruel spectacle of heat and despair. The sky glowed an eerie orange as the fire raged on. Helicopters from the nearest airbase had been summoned, their blades slicing through the smoky air, but they arrived too late. The inferno's intensity forced them back, its heat warping their hulls, rendering rescue impossible. They hovered helplessly above, ferrying the charred remains to the hospital below, their crews silent with the weight of failure.

The army, too, had been dispatched, but the terrain—a labyrinth of rocky slopes and dense, uncharted thickets—slowed their advance. Their boots sank into ash long after the screams had faded. Aircraft swooped low, spraying dousing chemicals that shimmered in the night like futile tears. But all these efforts were a belated elegy. The girls had already perished, their lives snuffed out by flames before the machines of salvation could reach them.

The doctors worked frantically, crafting stretchers from whatever they could find. Ten girls were carried down alive, their bodies ravaged by burns, their chances of survival slim. Ranji moved among the dead, his heart a leaden weight. He recognized fragments of clothing, a bracelet, a singed lock of hair—girls who had danced and laughed just hours before, now reduced to ash.

Three survivors emerged from the chaos—girls who had overslept and arrived at the pine tree after the fire had passed, and one who had clung to the tree itself, its branches shielding her from the blaze.

At the government hospital, Ranji stood among the stretchers, the cries of the injured echoing in his ears. The mortuary at Theni became a sombre theatre of grief as the bodies arrived, each shrouded in the grim silence of death, their blackened forms laid out on cold steel tables under the harsh glare of fluorescent lights. Families poured in, their faces etched with dread and disbelief, wandering from one gurney to the next in a desperate search for their daughters, sisters, nieces. Girls who had left home with dreams of adventure were now reduced to unrecognizable husks. The air was thick with wails and choked sobs, the agony of losing young family members cutting deeper than any blade, a pain that gnawed at the soul and left hearts hollow.

Meanwhile, ambulances raced through the night, their sirens piercing the chaos as they ferried the injured, those clinging to life with blistered skin and shattered spirits, to Madurai Medical College. There, doctors fought against odds. Yet despite their efforts, only two of the injured would eventually survive, the rest succumbing to wounds no medicine could mend.

Ranji could not shake the memory of the fire parting before him, a miracle he could not comprehend. Sleep eluded him, the weight of the day pressing down like a stone. He saw the faces of the dead, heard their screams, felt the heat of the flames that had spared him but taken so many.

The press swarmed, their cameras flashing and voices clamouring, turning the tragedy into a frenzied spectacle. Their questions drowned out the mourners' cries as the town buckled under the weight of sorrow and scrutiny.

The aftermath was a storm of its own. The fire made headlines, a tragedy that shook the nation. The government, desperate to contain the fallout, ordered an enquiry. The foresters who had neglected the fire lines, the fire brigade that arrived too late, the doctors absent from their posts—all had powerful allies to shield them.

Ranji, the orphan with no one to speak for him, became the scapegoat. Arrested and accused of negligence, he was branded a criminal, his heroism twisted into a tale of recklessness. The tribal boy who had saved lives was now a pariah, his name smeared across newspapers as the one who had led the trekkers to their doom.

In the quiet of his prison cell, Ranji sat with his head in his hands, the agony a wound that would never heal.

He had faced the fury of the flames, had carried a girl to safety and watched helplessly as others perished. The fun and frolic of that fateful evening felt like a distant dream, a cruel prelude to the drama of death that had unfolded.

The charred bodies, the failed rescues, the choppers that never came in time—all haunted him. Yet amidst the despair, he clung to the voices of the tribal lads who had aided him later, their simple courage a flicker of light in the darkness.

Ranji was now hallucinating. He was hearing voices. He was having vivid dreams.

'Ranji, you did what you could,' one of the rescuers had said, his voice rough but kind as they carried a stretcher down the hill. 'The fire was too big, too fast. No one could stop it.'

A doctor, weary and bloodstained, had nodded in agreement. 'You brought eleven out alive. That's more than most could have done. Do not let them tell you otherwise.'

But these words, though meant to comfort, could not erase the pain. Ranji was alone now, a man marked by fire, his fate twisted by the very hands he had sought to save. The agony of that day would linger forever, a scar etched into his soul—a testament to the fury he had faced, and above all, the lives he could not reclaim.

Chapter 9

The Truth beneath the Smoke

The forest fire had left scars—both on the land and in the memories of those who survived it. The smoke had long cleared from the hills, but questions lingered like stubborn ash. Who was to blame? Could it have been prevented? The government could not ignore the uproar. Newspapers screamed headlines, families demanded answers, the public wanted justice. So they set up a high-level enquiry committee. This was no mere formality; it was an attempt to dig deep, uncover the truth and recommend corrective measures, no matter where they led.

The chairman of the committee was an experienced IAS officer named Vijay. He was sharp, fearless and known for his refusal to bend under pressure. His dark eyes carried a quiet intensity, and his neatly pressed attire gave him an air of authority beyond his years.

Assisting him were two seasoned experts: Dinesh, a senior forest officer with a weathered face and a voice roughened by years in the wild, and Dr Priya, a wildlife expert with unmatched knowledge of forest habitats. Together, they formed a trio determined to leave no stone unturned.

The committee did not sit in air-conditioned offices flipping through reports. They rolled up their sleeves and trekked through the rugged terrain where the fire had raged. Vijay led the way, his boots crunching over charred earth, while Dinesh pointed out the natural firebreaks that had failed. Priya bent low to study the soil, her fingers sifting through ash to understand how the blaze had spread so fast. They walked for days, covering every inch of the affected area—from steep slopes to dense thickets, to the lone pine tree and along the winding trails where the trekkers had once laughed and chatted, unaware of the disaster to come.

Their first task was to determine what had sparked the fire. Was it a careless cigarette toss by a trekker? A lightning strike? Or something more sinister? They pored over weather reports, satellite images and soil samples.

Dinesh, with his decades of experience, had a hunch. 'Look at this,' he said one afternoon, crouching near a cluster of burnt shrubs. He held up a shard of glass glinting in the sunlight. 'A broken bottle can act like a lens, focusing the sun's rays. I have seen it before.'

Vijay nodded, scribbling in his notebook. It was not proof, but it was a clue. In the area, some estate owners were known to set fires in the dry grass to prepare fields for seasonal vegetables—a practice that could become dangerous if the winds set in.

Next, they tackled a larger question: why had the fire not been detected in time? The Forest Department had watchtowers, did it not?

Dinesh shook his head grimly. 'Understaffed,' he muttered. 'One man for three posts, and he is supposed to spot smoke through miles of trees?'

Priya added, 'And the fire lines—those cleared strips meant to block a blaze—were overgrown. No one maintained them this season.'

Vijay's jaw tightened. Negligence was piling up like dry tinder.

They did not stop at theories. The team hauled in everyone who might know something. Forest guards shuffled in, their uniforms rumpled and faces uneasy. Police officers gave clipped answers, dodging blame. Estate managers from nearby plantations shrugged, claiming they had seen nothing unusual. Tribal youth from the villages spoke in hushed tones, their eyes darting about nervously. Trekking organizers, slick and defensive, insisted they had followed every rule. Even the rescue teams from the defence forces, tough men in camouflage, sat down to recount the chaos of that day.

The committee set up a makeshift office in a forest rest house, the wooden walls creaking under the weight of their mission. Statements poured in, each one a piece of the puzzle. Vijay sat at a battered desk, his pen flying across pages as he listened. Dinesh leaned against the wall, arms crossed, while Priya asked pointed questions.

One tribal boy, barely eighteen, fidgeted as he spoke. 'We saw smoke, sir, but no one came when we shouted. The phone lines were down.' A forest guard admitted, 'I was at the tower, but the radio battery died. I could not call for help.' Little failures, stacked together, had turned a spark into a catastrophe.

Then came the survivors, all women, their voices heavy with what they had endured. Radha, the chess player, sat across from Vijay, her hands trembling but her voice steady. 'It was Ranji who saved us,' she said. 'The fire was everywhere, crackling, roaring, like a demon. We could not see, could not breathe. But Ranji...he kept shouting, "This way, this way!" He knew the paths. He carried me on his back when I fell.' Her eyes glistened. 'Eleven of us made it because of him.'

The others echoed her story. Anjali, a young teacher with her arm still bandaged, nodded vigorously. 'Ranji was like a madman—running back into the smoke to find more people. I thought he would die in there.'

An elderly woman, Mrs Ramanna, wiped her brow. 'I owe him my life. My legs gave out, but he dragged me to the plains.'

Every testimony painted the same picture—Ranji, the local guide, had been the hero of that horrific day.

Doctors and villagers who first reached the site added further layers. Dr Raj Kumar, a local physician with penetrating eyes and a no-nonsense tone, sat with Vijay one evening. 'We got there hours after it started,' he said, his voice clipped. 'The women were in shock—burns, smoke inhalation. Ranji was still pulling them out, covered in soot. He would not stop.'

A tribal elder named Rani, her voice raspy with age, told them, 'Our boys ran up with buckets and blankets, but the fire was too big. No officers came. There was no one to lead us. We did what we could.'

Vijay's pen paused. 'No officers?'

Rani shook her head. 'Not one. It was a long weekend. They were all in the city.'

The absence of senior forest officials gnawed at Vijay. This was not merely bad luck but a gaping hole in the system.

But there was a cruel irony. Ranji was not basking in any of this praise. He was in a jail cell, accused of negligence and blamed for leading the group into danger. The twist stung Vijay as he flipped through the arrest report. 'This does not add up,' he said one evening, tossing the file on to the table.

Dinesh raised an eyebrow. 'Do you think he has been made a scapegoat?'

Priya frowned. 'He is no expert, Vijay. He is just a guide. If the organizers did not brief him properly, how is this his fault?'

The more they dug, the clearer it became—Ranji was the fall guy in a long chain of institutional lapses, which included unmaintained fire lines, missing officers and trekking outfits more interested in glory than safety. Monitoring was a sham; no one had checked the risks.

Determined to get to the bottom of it, Vijay retraced Ranji's every step. He studied the trek route—a winding path through rocky cliffs leading all the way to a single pine tree, then descending to the tea estate. He met the Ecotourism Committee that employed Ranji—a group of tribal men who stumbled through their words.

'We trained him well,' one insisted, but the records were sketchy, more appropriate for local inhabitants than city dwellers unfamiliar with the terrain.

Vijay pressed harder, interviewing every trekker who had walked with Ranji that day. Their stories matched: Ranji had done everything he could.

The enquiry stretched beyond the hills. The team travelled to the Forest Research Institute in Dehradun, a sprawling campus of stone-grey imperial buildings nestled among deodar trees. There, they met fire experts who explained how dry leaves and unseasonal heat had turned the forest into a tinderbox.

'Prevention's the key,' one scientist said, tapping a map. 'Clear the undergrowth, train locals as spotters, ensure the forest beat is vigilant, install better communication lines.'

Vijay and his team scribbled furiously, ideas forming in their minds.

Back in the field, they met trekking promoters, enthusiastic folks who loved the wild. They admitted their flaws. 'We did not think a fire could spread so fast,' one woman said, twisting her dupatta. 'We need rules, training, something solid.'

Vijay agreed. The more he learned, the more convinced he became: this was not just about one fire. It was a deeply broken system.

The hardest part was meeting the families of those who had not made it. Vijay sat on a sofa in a middle-class flat in a suburban apartment in Chennai, facing a mother whose daughter had perished. Her eyes were red, her voice heavy with agony. 'She was new to trekking. Why did they not save her?'

Vijay had no easy answers, but he promised to find out the truth.

In another home, a sister clutched a photo of her sibling, her knuckles white. 'Someone must pay,' she whispered.

Vijay nodded. 'Someone should! We will also make sure it never happens again.'

Weeks turned into months. The committee's findings slowly began to take shape. They concluded the fire had likely started from a discarded glass bottle, its convex curve magnifying the sun's rays—a small mistake with massive consequences. But the inferno that followed was fuelled by bigger failures: overgrown fire lines, understaffed watchtowers, uncleared dry foliage, non-functional communication equipment and trekking groups sent out with little training. Senior officers had been absent, leaving juniors scrambling. The ecotourism boom had brought in money and crowd, but no one had prepared for the risks.

And then there was Ranji.

Vijay visited him in jail, a cramped cell with peeling paint and a single bulb flickering overhead. Ranji's face was etched with exhaustion, but his eyes held a quiet strength. 'I tried, sir,' he said simply. 'I could not leave them behind.'

Vijay leaned forward. 'Why did you go back into the fire?'

Ranji shrugged. 'It was my duty. They trusted me.'

That sealed it for Vijay. This was not negligence; this was courage.

The final report was a thick stack of pages, typed and bound, its message clear. Vijay presented it to the government with Dinesh and Priya at his side. 'Ranji saved eleven lives,' he said, his voice steady. 'He tried to save others too. He's no criminal. He deserves a gallantry award.'

The room buzzed with murmurs, but Vijay pressed on. 'And we cannot stop there. This fire exposed cracks in the system that need to be fixed.'

The recommendations were bold: first, absolve Ranji and honour him publicly; second, overhaul ecotourism. The committee proposed a safety toolkit. A detailed plan to prevent and fight forest fires. It included regular clearing of fire lines, more watchtowers with working communication equipment, binoculars and alarms, and trained local spotters from tribal communities. Trekking groups would need mandatory safety drills, fire extinguishers and guides certified in emergency response. Glass bottles, matchboxes and lighters were banned on treks. Every organizer would now submit a risk plan, checked by forest officials. Moreover, trekking needed to be prohibited in seasons when the forest was dry and prone to fire.

Vijay pictured it as he spoke: a network of vigilance, simple but strong. 'We can't stop every spark,' he said, 'but we can stop it from becoming a blaze.'

Dinesh added, 'Involve the villagers as they know the land better than anyone.'

Priya nodded. 'And educate trekkers. Make them part of the solution.'

Two months later, the government acted. Ranji walked out of jail, blinking in the sunlight as a crowd cheered.

'You are a hero,' Vijay told him, slapping his shoulder.

Ranji smiled faintly. 'I only did what I could.'

The safety toolkit rolled out across the hills. Fire

lines were cleared, radios crackled to life and guides like Ranji trained others. Ecotourism did not die, instead it grew safer and smarter. The forest healed, slowly, the green creeping back over the black. In the villages, people spoke of the fire not with fear, but as a lesson. They had faced the worst and come out stronger.

Vijay stood on a hilltop one evening, watching the sun dip below the trees. Dinesh joined him. 'Do you think it will work?' he asked.

Vijay smiled. 'It is a fair attempt. We have suggested the protocol. The rest is up to them.'

Below, the forest stretched wide, silent, resilient, ready for the next day.

TESTIMONY BY FIRE   85

Chapter 10

The Crown of Courage

anji's name echoed through the hills and beyond. His heroism in the forest fire was not merely a fleeting story. It became the talk of the town, then the district, and soon the whole state. The enquiry committee had peeled back the layers of that terrible day, and what they found shone like gold: Ranji's bravery, his unyielding spirit, his refusal to abandon the women trapped in the blaze. He was not just a guide any more. He was a symbol.

The government decided to honour him with the highest civilian award in the state, named after the revered former Chief Minister Annadurai, a man whose legacy of social justice still inspired millions. For Ranji, a simple man from a small hamlet, it was a dream he had never dared to dream.

The call came in July. Ranji was summoned to

Chennai for the Independence Day celebrations on 15 August. The government arranged everything—train tickets for him and one companion, a gesture of respect for the awardee. Ranji did not hesitate. He asked his old teacher, Murugan, to join him. Murugan, a lean man with greying hair and kind eyes, had been Ranji's rock at the Arts and Science College in Madurai. Years ago, when Ranji was just a boy with a big smile, Murugan had seen something in him.

'You are clever, Ranji,' he'd once said, setting up a chessboard on a rickety desk. 'This game teaches you to think ahead. Life's the same.' He taught Ranji the moves—pawn to king, strategy over haste—and cheered when Ranji won his first match. Now, Ranji wanted him there for this moment of glory.

They boarded the train at Madurai, a metre-gauge relic chugging its way from the southern districts to the grand city of Chennai. Ranji pressed his face to the window, watching the green hills fade into flat plains, then bustling towns. It was his first trip to Chennai, a city of which he had only heard about in stories, a city of tall buildings, endless roads and the sea, vast and alive. Murugan sat beside him, a small bag on his lap.

'Nervous?' he asked, his voice soft over the train's rattle.

Ranji grinned. 'A little. Mostly excited.'

Murugan chuckled. 'You've earned this, boy. Enjoy it.'

At Egmore railway station, a group of officials in crisp shirts greeted them, holding a sign with Ranji's name. The station was a marvel, its red-brick arches soaring overhead, voices echoing off the walls. Ranji clutched his bag, awestruck. They were whisked away in a government car to the state guest house near Marina Beach. The building was elegant, with white walls, wide verandas and a garden bursting with flowers. Ranji's room had a view of the grand Chepauk Stadium, which he had only heard of in radio commentary.

He dropped his bag and walked down to the beach. The sand was warm under his feet, the air salty and sharp. The Bay of Bengal stretched endless and blue, waves crashing against the shore with a rhythm that stole his breath. Ships dotted the horizon, their horns low and mournful, gliding towards the port. Iconic buildings lined the coast—the red and white lighthouse, Madras University with domes and spires, the old British-era offices, grand and weathered. Ranji had never seen anything like it.

Later, he sat with Murugan on a stone bench by the shore, watching the waves roll in, each one bigger than the last. Fishermen hauled nets in the distance, their boats bobbing like toys.

'It's alive,' Ranji said, almost to himself.

Murugan nodded, lighting a cigarette. 'The sea has got its own heartbeat. Like the forest, but wilder.'

They stayed until the sun sank, painting the water

gold, then purple. Ranji did not want to leave.

Ranji woke early next morning, nerves buzzing. Officials took him for a rehearsal. The arrangements were massive—orange, white and green flags flapping against the blue sky, policemen in starched uniforms rehearsing in perfect lines, their boots thumping the earth, the sound of brass and drums filling the air. Ranji stood in a corner, clutching the rehearsal schedule, feeling small but proud.

'Simply stand straight,' an officer told him, adjusting his collar. 'The compere will call your name.'

Ranji nodded, swallowing hard.

Independence Day dawned bright and loud the next morning. The beach road swelled with people— dignitaries in suits, families waving flags, children perched on shoulders. A siren wailed, sharp and sudden, cutting through the chatter. Motorcycles roared in, their engines growling, uniformed escorts circling an open jeep. The Chief Minister stepped out, a stout man in dark sunglasses, his face calm and commanding. The crowd erupted in cheers. Bugles blared, a deep, stirring sound, as the band struck up a patriotic tune. The parade began: soldiers, police and cadets marching in disciplined rows, rifles gleaming in the sun. It dwarfed the little NCC parades Ranji remembered from college. He watched, heart pounding, as the tricolour rose high, unfurling against the sky.

Then came the moment.

'For extraordinary bravery in the face of danger,' the announcer's voice rang out, 'we honour Ranjeeth Kumar with the Anna Award.'

The crowd clapped, the sound washing over Ranji like a wave. He walked forward—legs shaky, head high.

The Chief Minister smiled—a warm, familiar face Ranji had seen in grainy newspaper photos—and pinned the medal to his chest. It was heavy, gold and shining, with the government symbol and Anna's name etched in Tamil. He handed Ranji a citation, words of praise in bold ink, and an envelope with a cash prize of five lakh, more money than Ranji had ever imagined.

'You have made us proud,' the Chief Minister said, his voice deep and steady.

Ranji bowed. 'Thank you, sir. I only did my duty.'

The applause roared again, and Ranji felt it in his bones.

After the ceremony, they stayed one more day. Ranji wanted to see Radha, the shy, young girl whose testimony had turned the tide. She lived in a quiet Chennai suburb, a small house with a row of coconut trees in the backyard.

Radha opened the door, her eyes wide with surprise. 'Ranji sir!' she said, blushing. 'I did not think you would come.'

Inside, her room was simple. A desk, books and a chessboard by her bed. Ranji smiled. 'You continue to play?'

She nodded. 'Not as good as you, I bet.'

They laughed, and Ranji felt a warmth he could not name.

'You saved me too, Radha,' he said. 'Your testimony set me free.' She looked down, shy again. 'You deserved it.'

Back in Madurai, Ranji returned a hero. The District Collector, a stern man in well-ironed clothes, called him to the office. They sat in a room with a high ceiling and old wooden furniture, sipping tea from bone china cups.

'You are an example for us all,' he said, his tone formal but kind. Ranji nodded, still unused to the praise.

The Superintendent of Police, who had once locked him up, grinned widely, posing for a photo. 'Times change, eh?' he said, slapping Ranji's back. Ranji just smiled.

In Theni, Murugan led him to the post office, a small building with peeling paint and chatter in the queue.

'Open an account,' Murugan insisted. 'This money is your future.'

They set up a fixed deposit—five lakh locked in for six years, promising good interest.

'You will thank me later,' he said, winking.

Ranji laughed. 'I owe you already, sir.'

Back in Kurangani, his hamlet in the hills, the air smelled of tree resin and earth, familiar and sweet; elders greeted Ranji with watery eyes, children tugged at his shirt.

'Our Ranji!' an old woman cried, hugging him tight.

He had been gone for months—after the fire, the jail, the enquiry—and had now returned with honour. In his mud-walled house, he hung the citation and the photo with the Chief Minister on the veranda. The medal gleamed on a shelf in his room. Neighbours crowded in, touching it and whispering in awe.

Life did not stop, though.

Ranji went back to the ecotourism office the next week. The hills were greener now, healing. The place was the same but the air felt different.

Colleagues nodded at him, some with shy smiles. 'Big man now, huh?' one teased.

Ranji shrugged. 'Same job. Just louder applause.'

Days later, he sat with Murugan on a hill overlooking the valley. The sun dipped low, casting long shadows.

'What is next?' Murugan asked, puffing his cigarette.

Ranji stared at the horizon. 'Keep going, I guess. Teach others what I learnt.'

Murugan nodded. 'Good plan. Chess and life both ask you to think ahead.'

They sat in silence, the wind carrying the scent of the forest. Ranji's chest felt full—not just with the medal's weight, but with something bigger. He was home, and that was enough.

The honour had a ripple effect. Schools invited him to speak; children listened wide-eyed as he told his story. 'Be brave,' he would say, 'but be smart too.'

The ecotourism office framed his photo, a quiet boast to visitors. Newspapers ran features on Ranji calling him the 'Hero of Kurangani'. Strangers recognized him on buses, offering shy nods. The cash prize grew in the bank, a safety net he had not had before. But Ranji remained Ranji. Quiet, steady and rooted in the hills.

One evening, Radha wrote him a letter. 'I won my first chess tournament,' she had scrawled. 'Thank you for inspiring me.'

Ranji smiled, folding the paper carefully. He wrote back: 'Keep playing. You have the heart for it.'

The sea, the parade, the medal—they were grand, yes, but this felt just as real.

Months passed, and the Anna Award became a beacon. Local leaders cited Ranji in speeches as living proof of courage. The ecotourism toolkit rolled out stronger, his story its heartbeat.

Ranji watched it unfold, sometimes pinching himself. From a jail cell to a parade ground, from guide to hero, he had walked a path he could never have planned. As the forest grew back, so did he—step by step, wave by wave, move by move.

Chapter 11

Ashes of Glory

The Anna Award changed Ranji's life in ways he never imagined. It was not just the medal or the cash prize. The award opened doors that had always been locked for someone like him—a tribal boy from Kurangani. The government offered him a job as a forester, a foot soldier in the Forest Department, the one in charge of a beat. It was a role of responsibility. The job chart included counting tigers, elephants and wildlife, marking valuable trees, ensuring fire lines were cleared, removing encroachments on forest land and stopping trespassers.

For Ranji, it felt like a new chapter. The prestige of a government job wrapped around him like a warm blanket. He wore the green uniform with pride, the stripes on his shoulders gleaming under the sun. He was part of the system now, sharing space with high-ranking officers, standing in the chain of command. In his hamlet, he was a legend—the first one from his tribe to rise so high. Village elders, who once saw him as just another boy, now looked at him with awe and respect. Marriage proposals poured in, each one a testimony to his new-found status. Life, for the moment, seemed sorted.

However, every night, poignant memories replayed. He could feel Radha's weight, her warmth, and hear her soft breaths. Often, he would awaken in the midst of an emotional storm, tears streaming down his face, juxtaposed with a smile of gratitude and remembrance. The ordeal had shaped him, showing Ranji the depths of his strength and the fragility of life. While the external accolades celebrated his heroism, internally, Ranji grappled with the complexities of trauma and survival.

The shine of his coveted position dulled quickly. The Forest Department was a towering machine, and Ranji was just a small cog in its grinding wheels. The hierarchy was suffocating. Every report had to climb a rigid chain, from the lowest rung to the next, and the next, until it reached someone who might care or might not.

Ranji, diligent and earnest, wrote detailed reports about illegal tree cutting, poaching and unauthorized tapping of forest resources. He would trek deep into the woods, his boots sinking into damp earth, noting every felled tree, every suspicious footprint. But his words often vanished into the void. His superiors, sitting in air-conditioned offices, ignored them. No action, no response. Only silence. Ranji felt like a nut in a giant machine, helpless and unheard.

His knowledge of the forest, once his strength, became a burden. Officers called him along on their tours not for his insights but to carry their bags and show them the route. He would trudge behind them, a water bottle in one hand, a flask of tea in the other, their binoculars slung around his neck, biscuits rattling in a tin. The officers would point at a tree and ask its name, but never listened to his warnings about illegal felling or encroachments. The weight of their indifference felt heavier than the load he carried.

Ranji, quiet by nature, now kept to himself. He was not one for small talk or laughter over tea. He minded his own business, his eyes scanning the forest for signs of trouble, his heart sinking with every ignored report. The helplessness grew heavier each day, a stone in his chest.

Then came the day that broke him. Deep in the reserve forest, where the air was thick with the scent of wet leaves, Ranji stumbled upon a horrific sight. An elephant lay dead, its massive body slumped against a tree, its ivory tusks hacked off. The ground around it was stained dark with blood, flies buzzing in a frenzied cloud. The poachers had left it to rot, a majestic creature reduced to a carcass.

Ranji's stomach churned. He knelt beside it, his fingers brushing the rough skin, grief and anger swelling inside him. Ignoring this incident would revive elephant poaching, which had otherwise declined due to stern action and public outcry.

He waited for someone to come, to care. But no one did. His superiors wanted it hushed up, swept away like dust.

'Do not make a fuss,' a range officer told him over the phone, his voice cold. 'It is just one elephant. We are all going to be in trouble if this incident is reported.'

Ranji could not let it go. He spent days preparing a case, his hands trembling with purpose. He marked the site with stones, sketching its location on a map. Using his own savings, he hired a local photographer to take pictures, the shutter clicking as evidence piled up. Then, in a bold move, he wrote a detailed report and sent it straight to the State Wildlife Warden, bypassing the entire bureaucracy, including the Range Officer, the District Forest Officer and their superiors. He knew it was a risk, but he could not stay silent. The elephant deserved justice, and so did the forest.

The system turned on him like a predator. His defiance was a threat, and a lesson needed to be taught. A fabricated report on his conduct was prepared swiftly. They pinned charges on him like thorns: conniving with poachers, failing to clear fire lines, being discourteous, neglecting duties and refusing to cooperate with superiors.

Ranji stood before them, his uniform wrinkled from days in the field, his eyes steady but heart racing. He tried to explain, to show the photographs, to speak of the elephant. But they did not listen. Within days, a suspension order landed in his hands, the words cold and final. He was out, cast aside like a useless tool.

Ranji did not plead his innocence or appeal to higher-ups. He took the suspension order as a badge of honour—his first fight, his first sacrifice. He folded the paper carefully and tucked it into his bag. Then he walked away. He did not return to his hamlet, where the elders would look at him with pity. He did not go to the range office, where his desk sat empty. He vanished from the reserve forest—the place he had once called home. For a while, he stayed in the Ramakrishna Math, a quiet retreat where monks lived in silence. He sat under a banyan tree, the leaves whispering above him, and thought about his life. Before anyone could track him, he left, embarking on a pilgrimage with nothing but a small bag and a heavy heart.

He wandered across the state, living off temple prasadam— a frugal meal of pongal offered to devotees. He slept in the courtyards of temples, the cool stone beneath him, stars overhead. He found rest in the sanctity of churches, mosques, ashrams, and retreats, each place a brief shelter in his journey. Along the way, he met other wanderers—men and women with stories etched into their faces.

A sadhu with matted hair shared a fire with him one night. 'The world forgets, but the soul remembers,' he quoted, passing Ranji a chapatti.

An old woman at a mosque, her eyes tired but kind, gave him a blanket when the nights turned cold. 'You look like you are searching,' she said.

Ranji nodded. 'I do not know for what.'

His life became a myth, whispered in the places he passed through, a man who had fought for the forest and disappeared.

Meanwhile, the Wildlife Warden's office erupted in chaos.

Someone, perhaps a disgruntled colleague, had leaked Ranji's report to the press. Headlines screamed of corruption in the Forest Department. The public was furious. The department, meant to guard and nurture the forest, had turned it into a cash cow. Officers were hand in glove with poachers and encroachers, pocketing bribes while the wilderness bled.

The matter reached the State Legislative Assembly; lawmakers shouted over each other, demanding answers. The Wildlife Warden was quietly moved to an irrelevant post, a scapegoat for the storm. Many heads rolled. Officials who had suppressed Ranji's report were sacked. The officer who had framed charges against him was terminated from the job.

Ranji was reinstated, his suspension lifted with an official apology.

But there was no Ranji to receive the orders. He was gone, a ghost in the wind.

The department sent notices to his house, to the range office, to every address they could think of. They found nobody. Ranji had become a persona non grata, a name on a file, a memory fading with time. After its initial tremble, the department moved on. The incident was buried under layers of paperwork, an unopened file in the record room, gathering dust.

The world forgot Ranji, its attention shifting to new scandals and new headlines.

In his absence, the forest whispered his name. The trees he had marked stood tall; their bark scarred but strong. The fire lines he had fought for were cleared, a silent tribute to his battle. The elephant's death, though hushed at first, became a rallying cry for activists. A spark that lit reforms.

But Ranji did not see it. He was somewhere far away, walking a dusty road, the sun on his back, the weight of his choices lighter with each step. He had fought for what was right, and though the world had moved on, he carried the forest in his heart as a quiet, endless refuge no one could take away.

Chapter 12

Between the Squares of Silence

What happened in the years after Ranji disappeared from Kurangani remains a mystery to most. Few knew anything about him, and the little I could grasp felt like chasing smoke. The only thread tying him to the world was probably Radha.

I often wondered what held them together. Was it the quiet game of chess they played by a campfire, the flickering light casting shadows on the board? Or the moment he carried her on his back through the wild trails, her touch lingering in his memory? Perhaps it was her testimony—words spoken in a courtroom that pulled him from the edge of ruin, giving him a chance to live with dignity. Whatever it was, their bond ran like a deep current beneath the surface. The events that followed only thickened the haze around Ranji's life.

I started piecing things together, bit by bit, like assembling a mosaic from broken shards. Ranji used to receive letters at regular intervals. They arrived like clockwork: sometimes a thin envelope with a single page, other times a thick bundle, heavy as a booklet. He would sit with them for hours, reading carefully, his brow furrowed in thought. Then he would take up his pen and write a reply, his hand moving steadily across the paper.

I noticed a chessboard always lying next to his bed, its black and white squares worn from use. He would play for hours, moving pieces back and forth, lost in a world only he could see. There was a chess magazine he subscribed to as well, piled up in a corner, the pages dog-eared and yellowing. Every month, he would wait for the magazine, his eyes lighting up when it arrived, like a child unwrapping a long-awaited gift. I was curious, but I never pried. That was his space, a fortress he guarded fiercely.

Years later, when I helped him get his blue passport released after surrendering his diplomatic one, I could not believe what I saw. The pages were overflowing with stamps and visas from across the world—Australia, New Zealand, tiny islands in Oceania, small nations in South America and Africa. Where had he been? What had he been doing there? The questions gnawed at me, sharp and insistent.

I decided to call Radha as a last resort. It was a

long-distance call, and her voice crackled through the line, soft but guarded.

'Hello?' she said.

'Radha, it's me,' I replied, introducing myself and my connection to Ranji. It seemed she already knew who I was.

'I have been thinking about Ranji. There is so much I do not understand. Can you tell me anything?'

She paused, silence stretching between us. 'What do you want to know?'

'Everything,' I said, my voice almost pleading. 'The letters. The travels. What happened after Kurangani?'

She laughed lightly, a sound like wind through dry leaves. 'Everything? That's a tall order. Ranji's life is not easy to frame.'

'Just start somewhere,' I urged.

'All right,' she said. 'After Kurangani, he did not just vanish. He moved. Kept moving. He wrote to me often. Sometimes about where he had been, sometimes just thoughts. And chess moves.'

'Chess moves?' I asked, leaning forward.

'Yes,' she said. 'We played correspondence chess. One move at a time, sent by post. It could take months for a reply. Sometimes years for a game to finish.'

Correspondence chess is a slow, thoughtful way to play with someone far away. Instead of sitting across a board, players write their moves on paper and send them through the mail. Each move might take days, weeks or months to arrive. Then the other person thinks, writes their reply, and sends it back. A single game can stretch across years, with no rush, just quiet strategy. People keep a chessboard at home, shifting pieces as letters come, like a long-distance dance unfolding over time. It began before phones and computers, a way to connect across distances. For Ranji and Radha, it was the thread that held them together through his restless, itinerant life.

I leaned back, stunned. 'That's...incredible.'

'It was our way of staying connected,' she said. 'He'd write about other things too. People he met. Places he saw. But he never stayed still. And there were times— months, even years—when I would hear nothing. He would vanish, then reappear with a letter from some far-off place.'

'Where do you think he went?' I asked.

She sighed. 'Who knows! Some say he became a Naga sadhu. Those holy men who give up everything for the divine. They live in wild places—forests or mountains—smearing their bodies with ash, carrying tridents for Lord Shiva. Warriors of the spirit, half-myth to most. Maybe he tried that life, sat with them in silence, testing their ways. He never said.'

Her words painted a picture I had not expected. Ranji was not a man locked into one tale. He was a presence that flowed through the world, leaving traces in the form of letters, chess moves, passport stamps, whispers. I dug through what little I had of his life—a few diary pages he had left behind once, scribbled notes, half-finished thoughts.

One entry caught my eye: *Met K in the valley. Talked about the old ways. They are losing the forest. Must act.*

Another read: *R's last move was bold. Knight to E4. She's still sharp.*

I smiled at that. Radha's chess game with him lived in those pages, a quiet pulse beneath his wandering.

I found an old letter too, yellowed and creased: *I am in a village near the coast now. The people here fish with nets older than their grandfathers. They are losing the shore to big boats. I sat with them yesterday, listened. Tomorrow, we march. Your last move was clever, pawn to D5. I will think on it. Write soon.*

The letter was simple, but it held so much. I could see him there, seated on a sandy shore, the sea breeze tugging at his hair, planning a protest while pondering a chessboard move in his mind.

I called Radha again a few days later, the line buzzing with static. 'Did he ever talk about the coast?' I asked.

'Oh yes,' she said. 'He spent months there once. Helped the fishermen push back against the trawlers. He did not lead them, you know. He just connected them. Gave them a voice.'

'And the chess?' I pressed.

She laughed, warm and bright. 'Always the chess. He would send a move with every letter. Once he wrote, "You have trapped my bishop, but I will get your rook in three moves." I spent weeks figuring out if he was bluffing.'

'Was he?' I asked.

'No,' she said, a grin in her voice. 'He won that game. Took months, but he won.'

I could hear the fondness in her tone, a bond sustained through letters and slow games. His passport told a louder story: pages filled with stamps from places torn by struggle—remote islands where people fought for their waters, mountain villages where tribes battled for their habitat. He did not build an organization or lead a march. He was a field man, a wanderer who connected people to one another.

The more I learnt, the more his life felt like a puzzle with missing pieces. His diary held another note: *Spoke at the meet in J. They listened. Land's still theirs, for now.*

No place name, just 'J'. Maybe Jharkhand. But it had not even been formed then. Perhaps the tribals had always identified their abode as Jharkhand.

Then there was a crumpled flyer I found—a seminar on forest rights in Brazil. Ranji's name didn't appear on it, but the date matched the stamp in his passport.

I called Radha again, hungry for more. 'Brazil,' I said. 'Was he there?'

'Yes,' she said. 'He went to meet the indigenous groups. They were losing their rivers to dams. The rainforest was being razed to grow coffee and cash crops. He stayed a few months, connected them to lawyers. Sent me a move from there, queen to H3.'

'Always the chess,' I said, smiling.

'Always,' she replied. 'He would write about the people too. Said they reminded him of home. The hills and the forests. But then he would go quiet again. Weeks, months sometimes. I would wonder.'

'Wonder what?' I pressed.

'If he had joined the RSS,' she said. 'You know—the group that wants Hindu unity. They meet in *shakhas*, exercising, singing, waving their saffron flag. They are disciplined and rooted in tradition. Maybe he stood with them for a while, felt their pride, their order. He never told me.'

I nodded, picturing Ranji in a sea of brown shorts and white shirts, a lathi in hand, testing their ways before moving on. He was no longer just a man; he was becoming a legend. People whispered about him in villages and towns—tales of a Naga sadhu, perhaps, or an RSS wanderer. The myths grew in those silent stretches when even Radha didn't hear from him.

I sat in my study, surrounded by scraps: diary pages, a creased letter, a worn chessboard from his old room. Its squares were faded, the pieces chipped. A note beneath it read: *Radha, you got me in check. I will escape yet. King to F2.*

I smiled, imagining him hunched over it, plotting while the world churned. I called Radha again, craving more. The phone rang twice before she answered.

'It's me,' I said. 'How did your chess games start?'

She laughed softly. 'You are persistent, aren't you? It started after Kurangani. Before the fire or perhaps after it. He wrote me a letter from some village—his first since he had left. He must have been thinking about that night by the campfire, the game we played. He wrote, "Pawn to E4. Your move." I sent one back. And it just kept going.'

'How many games did you play?' I asked.

'I lost count,' she said. 'Some ended quickly. Others dragged on for years. One is still going. He sent me a move a while back, bishop to C5. I have not replied yet.'

I pictured her at a desk, a chessboard before her, puzzling over his challenge.

'Once, he wrote from an island in the Pacific,' Radha continued. 'The locals were fighting to keep their fishing waters. Another time, it was a forest in Africa, tribes losing their trees to loggers. He would tell me their stories, then slip in a move at the end.'

'Like a signature,' I said.

'Exactly,' she replied. 'It was his way of saying he was still out there. But those gaps—months, years with no word, I would wonder.'

I found another unposted letter, this one from a coastal town in South America: *Radha, I am with the fishermen here. The big ships are choking their nets. They marched yesterday, hundreds of them, shouting for their waters. It is like home, but hotter. Your last move was sneaky—rook to B7. I will get you yet. Write soon.*

The paper smelled of salt, as if the sea had seeped into it. I saw him there—sandals caked with sand, standing with weathered men as they faced the trawlers, a chess move his quiet tether to Radha.

I spread his passport across my desk, tracing the visas. Each mark was a story, a struggle he had touched. I called Radha again, my curiosity insatiable.

'He was in Botswana,' I said. 'And Ecuador. What was he doing there?'

'Same as always,' she said. 'In Botswana, he helped a tribe keep their grazing land. It seems some company wanted it for mining. In Ecuador, it was forest people fighting a dam. He stayed there for a few months, connected them to help, then moved on.'

'And the chess?' I asked, grinning.

'Never stopped,' she said. 'From Botswana, he wrote, "You are closing in—pawn to F6." From Ecuador, it was "King to G2". He would tease me, saying he would never let me checkmate him.'

'Did you?'

'Once,' she said, pride in her voice. 'Took years. He wrote back, "Well played. New game?"'

I laughed, picturing their rivalry spanning oceans. 'Did he ever talk about stopping?'

'Yes,' she said, her tone softening. 'Once, in a letter from New Zealand. He said, "Maybe I will come back someday. Finish a game by the fire." But he did not.

Sometimes I wondered if he had turned Naxalite. You know, those rebels in the forests, fighting with guns for the poor. They hide, striking at the powerful, claiming justice for tribals and farmers. Maybe he walked their path for a time, felt their anger.'

I could see it—Ranji in the shadows of a jungle, listening to their plans, weighing their cause before slipping away. The myths multiplied: a sadhu in the hills, an RSS wanderer, a Naxalite in the wild. I tracked down more voices.

In Assam, an activist named Deepak remembered meeting him at a tea stall, his shirt crumpled, eyes tired but sharp.

'Ranji came here once,' he said, stirring his tea. 'Tea garden workers were losing their wages. He sat with us, asked questions. Next week, we rebelled. He was gone by then, but we won.'

'No speeches?' I asked.

'No,' Deepak said. 'He listened. Connected us to a union. Quiet guy.'

In Tamil Nadu, I found a fisherman, Mariappan, by his nets, his hands rough as the rope he mended. 'He came when the trawlers started,' he said. 'Showed us how to block the harbour. Taught us to speak as one. Left before the officials came.'

In Odisha, an elder named Birsa sipped water from a clay cup under a banyan tree. 'He was here. Spoke for our forest. Brought a lawyer from the city. Soft voice, but it carried.'

Every tale was the same. Ranji appeared, connected and vanished. He never created headlines. He was just a ripple that grew.

I called Radha one last time, the line faint with distance.

'Did he ever chase anything spiritual?' I asked. 'Beyond groups, just...the divine?'

'Maybe,' she said. 'There were times he wrote about the stars, about the silence of the forest at night. Maybe he sat alone, seeking something bigger. But he always came back to the people. The poor, the tribals, the aboriginals—they were his canvas.'

That day, I found an old chess set in his room—pieces worn, board scratched. The note beneath it, *King to F2*, felt like a whisper from him. I pictured him sitting there, alone but not lonely, plotting his next move.

I sat at my desk with all I had gathered: diary pages, letters, passport stamps, hearsay. I wrote and wrote until I had nothing more to narrate.

Ranji might have walked with sadhus, stood in shakhas, slept in rebel camps, or sought the divine. He did not reject those paths—he moved through them, always returning to the margins. To the poor, the tribals, the aboriginals. Their problems were his fight, silent but firm. His life was in the margins: a chess move on paper, a visa stamp, a name whispered in gratitude. And as those whispers grew, so did his enigma. Ranji was a man, real and everywhere.

Chapter 13

The Accidental President

anjeeth's past was a puzzle pieced together from scattered fragments. His letters, scribbled notes in a worn diary, and the chess moves he recorded on a crumpled sheet were all that remained to tell his story. There were no photographs to capture his face, no recordings of his voice, no family or friends to share tales of his life. He walked alone, a solitary figure moving through the world with quiet determination. Yet his presence was undeniable.

He never led a protest or built an organization. Instead, he travelled, joined in, and stood among the people as one of them—ordinary yet constant, patient yet passionate. Wherever the aboriginals, native people or tribals gathered for a cause, Ranjeeth was there— silent but always present. Over time, his persistence drew notice. The tribals, the forgotten voices of India, began to see him as one of their own. He did not shout from podiums or wave flags, but his steady presence spoke louder than any speech. Slowly, he emerged as a symbol—a quiet representative of a group long ignored. In a country where every vote bank mattered, this shift carried weight.

Indian politics was changing. The old rules no longer held firm. Pressure groups, once sidelined, now shaped the game. Communities, castes, religions—none could be taken for granted. Elections were growing tighter, margins razor-thin. A handful of votes was enough to tip the scales. Politicians could no longer rely on fiery speeches or grand promises alone; people now demanded schemes, projects and, most of all, representation—a seat at the table, a share of the power.

The country stood at a crossroads. Assembly elections loomed in several states, the stakes towering high. A string of losses could trigger a nationwide shift, threatening the ruling party's grip on the government. Years in office had bred incumbency and resentment. Unemployment gnawed at the economy; inflation squeezed the common man. They needed something bold to turn the tide. The tribals, a vast and vital vote bank, held the key. The opposition was gaining ground in those regions, chipping away at the ruling party's bastion. Every move mattered.

At the same time, the President of India's term was nearing its end; the post would soon fall vacant. By tradition, the Vice President was next in line, but this was no ordinary moment. Another custom lingered: it was the South's turn to claim the presidency. The ruling party saw a chance to rewrite the script. Strategists huddled in closed rooms, voices low but urgent, searching for a candidate who could unify, not divide—someone from the tribal community who might sway the tribal vote and shore up their crumbling support. A controversial name might fracture their coalition; picking one state over another could alienate entire regions. They needed consensus, a name above the fray.

That was when Ranji's name surfaced.

At first, it seemed absurd. He had never stepped into active politics, held no party membership, won no election or delivered any grand speeches. The idea was dismissed outright.

'Who is this man?' some scoffed.

'A nobody,' others muttered.

But the idea lingered like a seed in dry soil.

Days later, a senior leader returned to it, pacing the room. 'He is clean,' he said. 'No enemies. The tribals know him. The South will like it.'

Others nodded slowly, the maths clicking into place. Tribal votes could tilt the state elections; a southern tribal president could help seal the deal. Word spread quietly but quickly through party ranks. Soon, Ranjeeth's name was on every tongue.

As whispers grew louder, he emerged as a dark

horse: an outsider with no baggage, a silent crusader who had walked among the tribals for years without ever seeking power or praise. No one disliked him, no scandals trailed him, and he fit the moment perfectly.

The President was largely a ceremonial figure, a notional head of state, not a rival to the political executive. Ranjeeth, with his quiet ways, seemed ideal; he was unlikely to challenge the Prime Minister or stir any trouble. He would play his part and stay in the shadows.

The Vice President, sensing the shift, tried to push back, his voice tight with frustration. 'This is my turn,' he insisted, but the party had decided. They sat him down, explained the stakes, and gently urged him to step aside. Reluctantly, he bowed to the inevitable.

Ranjeeth's name was set.

They tracked him down in a small village in Tamil Nadu, where he sat under a banyan tree, sipping tea with farmers. A party emissary approached, nervous but firm.

'Sir, we need to talk,' he said.

Ranjeeth looked up, his dark eyes calm. 'About what?' he asked, his voice soft but steady.

'The presidency,' the man replied. 'We want you to run.'

Ranjeeth set his cup down, his brow furrowing. 'Me? I'm no politician.'

'That's why,' the emissary said. 'You are one of them. The people. They trust you.'

Ranjeeth said nothing for a long moment, staring first at the ground, then at the faces around him, as if listening to something only he could hear. The farmers watched, curious but silent. Even the birds seemed to hush. Finally, he nodded. 'If they want me, I'll do it,' he said simply.

That was all it took.

A few days later, Ranjeeth sat alone in a modest guest house room, pulled out his diary, its pages yellowed and frayed, and wrote: *They chose me today. I do not know why. I never asked for this. But if it helps them, I'll try.*

He closed the diary, set it aside and lay down to sleep.

The opposition scrambled to respond, left with little choice but to accept the game being played. They fielded a veteran politician—a seasoned face with decades in the ring—against Ranji, but the numbers were not there. The presidential election rested in the hands of Members of Parliament and state legislators, and Ranjeeth, the humble tribal, was untouchable.

To oppose him openly would backfire, painting them as elitists trampling on a man of the people. They grumbled in private, but their resistance faded.

Ranjeeth was elected President of India with a sweeping margin, a victory that stunned even those who had proposed his name.

Chapter 14

The Silent Head of State

The Ashoka Hall of Rashtrapati Bhavan shimmered with quiet grandeur on the day Ranji took his oath as President of India. With its high ceilings, golden chandeliers and polished marble floors, the hall stood as a testament to the nation's past. Yet the ceremony itself felt subdued, almost like a formality tucked away from the public gaze. Rows of chairs held a modest gathering: the Prime Minister, a few ministers, the leader of the opposition, senior bureaucrats and a handful of tribal leaders. The air carried a faint trace of sandalwood, and the low hum of anticipation filled the space as Ranji stepped forward.

He wore a simple hand-spun white shirt, a veshti with an angavastram draped over his shoulder. His greying hair was neatly combed back. His face, weathered by years under the sun, carried no trace of excitement or pride. Instead, his eyes held a quiet unease, as if he already sensed the weight of the role he was stepping into.

Chief Justice Meera Kapoor stood before him, her black robes stark against the hall's opulence. She held the oath paper in her hands, her voice steady as she read the words aloud. Ranji repeated them in a low, measured tone: 'I, Ranjeeth Kumar, son of Muthu, do swear in the name of God that I will faithfully perform my duties as the President of India and will, to the best of my ability, preserve, protect and defend the Constitution and the law...'

The words echoed briefly before fading into stillness.

A smattering of applause followed, polite and restrained. The Prime Minister, seated in the front row, rose to shake Ranji's hand. His broad smile and firm grip seemed to overshadow Ranji's smaller frame. Cameras clicked, capturing the moment, but there was little real buzz. The press, stationed at the back, scribbled with mild interest. To them, Ranji's election was merely a political manoeuvre, a nod to the tribal vote bank rather than a triumph of merit. His past as a minor tribal activist offered no juicy headlines. The tribal communities celebrated quietly in their villages, but Ranji was no messiah to them. He was just a familiar face elevated by chance.

After the oath, Ranji signed the register, his hand slow but steady. He glanced up at the portraits of past presidents lining the walls. Their stern gazes seemed to study him, as though questioning his place among them. A brief reception followed in the Durbar Hall, where tea and samosas were served. Dignitaries approached him with practised smiles, offering congratulations that felt more like protocol than warmth. 'A historic day for the tribals,' a senior minister said, slapping Ranji on the shoulder.

Ranji nodded, his lips curving into a faint smile. 'Thank you,' he murmured, his voice barely audible over the chatter.

That evening, Ranji retired to his new residence: a single room within the sprawling Rashtrapati Bhavan. The 340-room mansion, with its endless corridors and manicured gardens, dwarfed his simple existence. He chose a modest chamber on the first floor, overlooking a quiet courtyard. The room had a wooden bed, a small desk and a shelf for his books—mostly worn-out volumes on tribal folklore, nature and, yes, chess. The rest of the mansion remained untouched by his presence, its grandeur a stark contrast to his frugal life. He owned no fancy suits, no ornaments, no entourage to fill the space. There was no First Lady, no children, no relatives in tow. Ranji was alone, a solitary figure in a palace built for pomp.

As President, his duties were clear but hollow. As the head of state, he was a constitutional figurehead—a guardian of the nation's laws and a symbol of unity, expected to sign bills into law, appoint governors and judges, and address the nation on occasions. Yet in practice, his powers were limited, overshadowed by the towering presence of the Prime Minister and the political executive. Every decision, every word, came scripted from the government—a rubber stamp in a system that moved without his input.

His days settled into a predictable rhythm. Mornings began with a cup of tea and a walk in the Mughal Gardens, where he watched birds flit between the rose bushes. By nine, his secretary and other staff arrived with a stack of files. There were bills to sign and appointments to be approved. Ranji would read each one carefully, his brow furrowing at the dense legal language, but he knew his signature was all that mattered.

'Anything I should know here?' he would often ask, holding up a thick document.

The secretary would smile thinly. 'Just routine, sir. The Cabinet has already cleared it.'

Ranji would nod and sign, the pen scratching against the paper like a whisper of surrender.

Ceremonies filled his calendar—welcoming foreign leaders beneath the grand portico, pinning medals on soldiers' chests whose eyes shone with pride as they stood atop the saluting base, tanks rolling past and jets streaking overhead. The crowd cheered while Ranji's face stayed calm, almost distant.

'This is for them,' he told an aide once, gesturing to the masses. 'Not me.'

At night, he found solace in his chessboard, moving its pieces—worn from years of play—replaying old games from memory.

One evening, an aide spotted him at it. 'Sir, do you play?' the young man asked.

'Not really,' Ranji replied, sliding a pawn forward.

His public appearances were few and tightly choreographed. The joint sessions of Parliament were the grandest, held in the Central Hall with its domed ceiling and rows filled with Members of Parliament (MPs). Ranji stood at the podium, a prepared speech in his hands, and read in a soft, monotonous voice: 'The government is committed to progress and unity...' he intoned, his words drifting over the restless audience.

Some MPs listened; others shuffled papers or whispered among themselves. The speech, written by the Prime Minister's Office, was a dry summary of policies he had no hand in shaping. When he finished, the applause was tepid, and he returned to his seat, dwarfed by the Prime Minister's commanding presence beside him.

Republic Day was no different. On 26 January, Ranji sat in the presidential box on Rajpath, watching the parade unfold. Floats rolled by, soldiers marched in perfect sync, folk dancers twirled in vibrant costumes. The crowd cheered, but their eyes were on the Prime

Minister, who waved confidently from the stage.

Ranji, in his simple coat, seemed to fade into the background, a quiet observer in a sea of spectacle. The cameras lingered on him for a moment, then moved on. He clapped when expected, smiled when prompted, but inside, he felt like a guest at someone else's celebration.

Weeks turned into months, and the monotony settled over Ranji like dust. Every day mirrored the previous: tea, files, a brief meeting or two, then silence. His interactions with dignitaries were short and mechanical. A foreign delegation would arrive, they would pose for a photo, exchange pleasantries and part ways.

'A pleasure to meet you, Mr President,' they would say.

'Likewise,' Ranji would reply, his voice flat. The conversations never deepened; there was no room for that. His role demanded brevity, not substance.

He rarely travelled overseas, and when he did, it was to places others overlooked. No grand tours of Europe or America for him. Instead, he visited small nations, countries off the beaten path, where he could escape the spotlight. In Vanuatu, he walked barefoot along a beach with local elders, listening to their stories of the sea. In Tanzania, he sat under a baobab tree, watching elephants roam. These trips were brief, unpublicized, and spent mostly among the Indian diaspora, nature and indigenous people. The press barely noticed and the government did not care.

'Let him have his little adventures,' one aide reportedly said.

For Ranji, these moments were a rare breath of freedom, a glimpse of the life he had once known.

In Delhi, Rashtrapati Bhavan, with its endless staff and protocol, felt like a gilded prison. He longed for the simplicity of his village: the mud walls, the open sky, the chatter of his friends. Here, every move was watched, every word weighed. He could not deviate from the script, could not speak his mind. Once, during a meeting with the Prime Minister, he tried to raise a concern. 'The tribal lands in Madhya Pradesh are shrinking,' he said, his voice tentative. 'The forests are dying too. Can we do something?'

The Prime Minister leaned back in his chair, a faint smile on his lips. 'We're looking into it. These things take time.'

The ministers around the table nodded vaguely, and the topic dissolved. Ranji sat back, his hands folded, feeling the weight of their indifference.

He tried again a few months later, during a reception for environmentalists. 'The rivers are drying up,' he said to a group of officials, his tone earnest. 'The Adivasis depend on them.'

A junior minister chuckled lightly. 'You are above politics, sir. We will address this issue.'

The rebuke was gentle but firm, a reminder of his place. Ranji's shoulders slumped and he retreated into silence. His role, he realized, was ornamental. He was a tribal face to parade when convenient, a voice to mute when it dared to speak.

At a state dinner, surrounded by crystal glasses and silver cutlery, he leaned towards the Prime Minister. 'Do we need all this?' he asked, gesturing at the table.

The Prime Minister chuckled. 'It's tradition. People expect it.'

Ranji nodded but his eyes lingered on the excess. He later wrote in his diary: Too much shine. I miss the earth under my feet.

Yet he grew into the role, and his rare speeches began to carry weight. At a tribal conference, he stood before a thousand faces and said, 'You are India. Never forget that.' The room thundered with applause, his chest swelling slightly though he did not smile. He was their voice and he knew it.

In the vastness of Rashtrapati Bhavan, Ranji's needs remained small. He ate simple meals—sambar, curd, rice and a vegetable curry—served on a steel plate in his room. The staff offered lavish spreads, but he waved them away. 'This is enough,' he would say, his voice quiet but firm. He wore the same few shirts, washed and pressed by the attendants, and kept his belongings to a minimum. A pair of worn sandals, angavastrams and his books were all he claimed as his own. The rest of the mansion along with its chandeliers, silk curtains and gold-trimmed furniture belonged to someone else's world.

Once, a young aide named Muskan brought him a tray of tea. 'Sir, why do you never ask for anything, something more?' she asked, curiosity breaking through her usual reserve.

Ranji set his cup down and looked at her. 'More of what, beta? I have a bed, food, a roof. That is more than I ever had growing up.'

Muskan frowned, unsure how to respond. 'But this is Rashtrapati Bhavan,' she said. 'It is meant for grand things.'

Ranji chuckled softly. 'Maybe. But I am not a grand man.'

She left, puzzled, and he sipped his tea, the steam rising in lazy curls.

He wrote letters too, though few knew it, sending handwritten notes to tribal leaders and an old lady friend. He also received correspondence in stacks: pleas for schools, roads and water. He passed them to the government, saying little.

'They should see this,' he would tell his secretary, and that was that.

Chapter 15

The Quiet Crusader

Ranji sat in his small room in Rashtrapati Bhavan, the morning sun spilling through the window on to his wooden desk. It was late in his presidency, and the weight of his role pressed heavier than ever. He was the first citizen of India, head of the Army, Navy and Air Force, and held the power to pardon death sentences. He had a full train at his disposal, a palatial mansion, countless staff and protocol privileges that followed him like a shadow. Yet these were trappings—hollow symbols of a position that offered no real sway. The Constitution painted him as a titan, but in practice he was a figurehead, a ceremonial puppet dancing to the tune of the Prime Minister and the political executive. His signature on bills meant nothing beyond a formality. His voice, when he dared to raise it, dissolved into the air like mist.

The presidency came with opportunities, but it also brought barriers. Protocol dictated his every move, security cordons kept him at a distance and layers of bureaucracy muffled his voice. Ranji needed a way through this maze, a bridge to the real India beyond the marble walls.

He refused to let his presidency drift into irrelevance. He wanted to do something substantial, something that mattered, even within the confines of his gilded cage. The pomp and perks were superfluous to him; he craved purpose. His early attempts to intervene on issues relating to tribal rights and environmental decay had fallen flat, met with polite smiles and no action. Still, he was not ready to surrender. He began to search for a way to be useful, to leave a mark that was not just a name etched in history books. He started a new trend, a quiet rebellion against the monotony of his office.

He turned his gaze to the 543 members of the Lok Sabha, each representing a constituency, a part of the nation's vast canvas. Then there were the 245 members of the Rajya Sabha, a pool of experience, ideologies and expertise, refreshed every two years with new faces. Together, they were a mammoth resource, a living link to the country's heartbeat—its culture, cuisine, grassroots struggles, hidden potential, untold stories.

Ranji decided to meet them, one by one, in an informal setting. He would invite an MP to Rashtrapati

Bhavan each morning at six, when the city still slept and the air carried a gentle chill. The day began with a warm cup of tea served in the courtyard, steam rising from cups as the first light touched the roses in the Mughal Gardens. Then came a long walk through the sprawling estate, a chance for Ranji to explore every nook and corner of his vast preserve while listening to his guest. The stroll ended with a simple breakfast of idli, dosa and a bowl of fruit, laid out on a table under a neem tree. These meetings were his window to the world, a way to connect with the people through their elected voices.

At first, the MPs were wary. They were used to being governed by a whip. 'Is this politicking?' each wondered after leaving the mansion. But suspicion faded as word spread. Ranji was not playing games; he was reaching out. For each meeting, he prepared meticulously. His desk overflowed with notes: maps of constituencies, reports on local issues, snippets of history and tradition. He read about the legends tied to each place, the monuments crumbling in neglect, the skills of artisans, the quiet resistance brewing in villages. When the guest arrived, he steered the conversation with care, asking questions, listening intently and nudging them back to their constituencies whenever they drifted to Delhi's power games.

One morning, he welcomed Sunita Devi, an MP from a dusty district in Rajasthan. She arrived in a colourful sari, her eyes sharp with curiosity. They sat with their tea, the garden waking around them.

'Tell me about your people,' Ranji said, his voice soft but firm.

Sunita smiled faintly. 'They're tough, sir. The desert makes them that way. But water is the problem—wells dry up and the canals never reach us.'

Ranji nodded, his fingers tracing the rim of his cup. 'What do they do then?' he asked.

'They dig deeper,' she said. 'Or they leave. The young ones go to cities, and the villages shrink.'

They walked past the fountains, the sound of water a cruel irony to her words. 'What could help?' Ranji pressed.

Sunita thought for a moment. 'Tanks to store rainwater. And pipes that actually work. We have plans, but the funds vanish somewhere.'

Ranji listened, his face still, absorbing every detail.

During breakfast, she spoke of the weavers in her district, their hands crafting rugs no one bought any more. 'There is talent there,' she said, 'but no market.'

Ranji chewed his idli slowly, trying to grasp everything she said.

Another day, it was Nikhil Patel from a coastal town in Gujarat. The tea steamed as they sat, the sea breeze a distant memory in Delhi's stillness. 'Fishing's our life,' Nikhil began, his voice rough. 'But the big boats take everything. Our nets come back empty.'

Ranji leaned forward. 'What do the fishermen want?' he asked.

'A limit,' Nikhil said. 'Keep the trawlers out of our waters. And maybe some cold storage so the catch does not rot.'

They walked through the herb garden. Ranji pointed at a patch of mint. 'This grows anywhere,' he said.

Over breakfast, Ranji asked about the town's salt pans, its crab catchers, its forgotten temples. Nikhil left with a grin, surprised by the President's quiet curiosity.

After each meeting, Ranji retreated to his room, a notebook in hand. He wrote long, detailed reports—pages of cramped handwriting capturing the essence of every constituency. For Sunita's district, he noted the water crisis, the dying wells, the weavers' plight. He suggested rainwater tanks, a craft fair, a survey of broken canals. For Nikhil's town, he recorded the fishermen's struggles, the need for storage, the call for fishing zones. Each report ended with specific recommendations—practical ideas born from hours of listening. He stayed clear of policy or politics, focusing instead on local potential, on what could be if someone cared to act.

The Presidential Secretariat typed these reports and sent them to the Cabinet Secretariat. A week later, an acknowledgement arrived: 'Received with thanks.' Nothing more. There were no action-taken reports and absolutely no follow-up. Ranji did not expect miracles; he knew his words carried hardly any weight in the machinery of government. But he had made a point. These reports were recorded, registered, filed away in the archives of power. They were seeds planted in barren soil, waiting for a day when someone might dig them up and see their worth. He imagined a future researcher, a young Member of Parliament, or even a villager stumbling across them, finding inspiration in the pages he had left behind.

One evening, as he finished a report on a hilly constituency in Uttarakhand, the secretary knocked on his door.

'Sir, why do you bother?' the secretary asked, his tone gentle but puzzled. 'They do not listen. The Cabinet just stacks these away.'

Ranji looked up, his pen pausing. 'Maybe they do not listen now,' he said, 'but it is there. Some day, it might matter. I cannot stop trying.'

The secretary sighed, adjusting his glasses. 'You are a strange man, sir. Most would give up.'

Ranji smiled faintly. 'I am not most. I am just me.'

The secretary left, and Ranji returned to his writing, the lamp casting a soft glow over his work.

Mornings became the heartbeat of Ranji's presidency. When he was in Delhi, nothing else mattered as much. The meetings ended before the city stirred, before the ceremonial duties and imperial protocols swallowed his day. By nine, he was back in his room, the guest gone, the notes piling up. The rest of his schedule—signing files, hosting dignitaries, reading speeches—felt like shadow play. But those early hours were real, a lifeline to the nation he served but could not shape.

Through these talks, India unfolded before him. He learnt of the millet farmers in Madhya Pradesh, their crops wilting under erratic rains. He heard of the silk weavers in Assam, their looms silent without buyers. He discovered the shepherds of Himachal, their pastures shrinking as roads crept higher. He saw the honey collectors of the Sundarbans, the potters of Kutch and the dancers of Manipur. Each story added to his understanding, equipping him for a role he could not yet define. He noted murmurs of resistance, the quiet anger in places ignored by Delhi's glare. He traced the threads of history, from ancient forts to colonial scars, and marvelled at the traditions holding strong against time.

One morning, he met Meenakshi Shankar, an MP from a tribal belt in Odisha. They walked past the peacocks strutting in the garden, her voice steady as she spoke. 'Our forests are gold, sir,' she said. 'Medicinal plants, timber, streams. But the mines take it all.'

Ranji stopped, watching a bird peck at the grass. 'What do your people need?' he asked.

'Control,' she said. 'Let us manage the forests. And schools—our kids walk miles for one.'

At breakfast, she told him of a festival where they

danced with feathers, a ritual older than the hills. Ranji wrote it all down later, his report brimming with ideas: community forest rights, mobile classrooms, a market for herbal cures. He knew it would lie unread, but he sent it off anyway.

The MPs began to enjoy these visits. It was a rare chance to sit with the President, the first among equals, in a space free of cameras and posturing. They peeked into the mansion's corners—the library with its leather-bound books, the veranda with its view of Lutyens' Delhi, the kitchen where staff brewed tea. Some left with a sense of awe, others with a quiet respect for Ranji's focus.

'He's different,' one MP told a colleague. 'Does not care about power. Just listens.'

'I thought he would lecture me. Instead, he asked me about my goats,' the other replied, laughing.

Ranji never drifted. He kept the talks grounded in the constituencies, steering away from Delhi's gossip or partisan jabs. If an MP veered into politics, he would smile and say, 'Tell me about your rivers instead,' or 'What grows in your fields?'

His guests obliged, drawn by his patience and genuine interest. He became an authority on India's remote reaches, a keeper of its secrets. He knew vivid details of the floods of Bihar, the droughts of Vidarbha, the winds of Ladakh. He understood the dreams of a potter in Tamil Nadu, the fears of a fisherman in Kerala.

It was a knowledge no one asked for, but he built it anyway, brick by brick.

Once Ranji asked an MP why these issues never came up in Parliament. 'Why is the discourse only on trivial issues along party lines? Why only big industries and large projects?'

'Because that matters more. People are sick and tired of their old ways, and want economic growth and industries,' the MP replied.

Ranji noted it in capital letters, drawing a bold underline underneath.

As his term neared its end, Ranji sat one evening with his stack of notebooks. Hundreds of reports lined his shelves, a silent testament to his mornings. He ran his fingers over the pages, feeling the weight of the stories they held. He had not changed the nation; he had not moved the needle on policy or power. The Cabinet ignored his work, the Prime Minister smiled and nodded, and the bureaucracy churned on. Yet, he had done something. He had seen India. Not the India of headlines or speeches, but the India of its people. He had recorded their stories, preserved then, left it for a day when they might matter.

'Will anyone read these?' I asked him once, sitting across from him in his room. The air smelled of ink and old paper.

Ranji looked at me, his eyes tired but clear. 'Maybe not today,' he said. 'Maybe not tomorrow. But they are there. That is enough.'

I nodded, struck by his quiet resolve. 'You could have stopped,' I said. 'Why did you not?'

He leaned back, gazing at the ceiling. 'Because I am still here,' he said. 'As long as I am, I will try. Even if it is just this.'

Once, I asked why he was limiting himself. 'You are the President,' I said. 'You can break protocol and create ripples. You did it once as a humble forester.'

'The framers of the Constitution created systems,' he replied after a pause. 'Systems strong enough that even a bad coin cannot distort them beyond a point. There are checks and balances and I will be the last one to break them.'

His presidency remained notional, ceremonial. But in those early mornings, in the walks and talks and scribbled notes, Ranji found a purpose. He wove an epic of India's soul, thread by thread, and left it waiting. A legacy no one saw coming, a gift for a future he would not live to see.

Chapter 16

The Endless March

Ranji's journey had woven itself into India's fabric, a legend murmured from dusty hamlets to crowded cities. The former president—the walking ghost who rose from the whispers of his pyre—roamed the nation on foot: a silent figure offering no answers, no words, no hints of purpose. Behind him trailed a crowd: volunteers drawn like moths to his flame, security men with clenched jaws, journalists wielding microphones, students clutching notebooks, and onlookers gripped by the enigma of his path. Some walked a few kilometres before slipping away, their legs tired or interest spent. Others lingered, drawn deeper into his spell. But a few stayed close, shadows to his silence, unable to abandon the man who refused to fade away.

His routes defied reason, a maze no map could trace. He skipped the Taj Mahal's polished glory but lingered in Fatehpur Sikri, a Mughal city lost to thirst, its red sandstone palaces baking under a relentless sun. Built by Akbar centuries ago, it was a marvel of symmetry—palaces with carved screens, a mosque with soaring arches, a tomb where pilgrims tied threads for luck... But the wells dried, the rivers shrank and the city emptied, its splendour left to crumble.

Ranji bypassed Hyderabad's clamour to tread through Daulatabad, a forgotten capital built to replace Delhi. Its broken walls stood as a monument to a king's folly. Muhammad bin Tughlaq dreamed it as a new seat of power, forcing people from their homes to settle in harsh terrain. But the water was scarce, the soil unforgiving, and the displaced cursed their fate. A Sufi saint, they say, doomed it to house only jackals, leaving it a shell of stone.

He sought places where faith called millions— Shaktipeeths alive with the power of goddesses, Shivalingams kissed by rivers, Lord Vishnu temples ringing with devotion, grand churches with arched roofs, mosques humming with prayer, Sufi shrines fragrant with song, Jain temples carved in stillness, Buddhist viharas steeped in calm, ashrams and retreats hidden in quiet corners. He also slipped into slums, paused at artisans' thresholds, stood among potters shaping clay. His path curved into the fringes—borderlands where nations blurred, Naxalite forests thick with danger, hills shadowed by terror. There his security tightened, their voices sharp and their hands restless on radios. But Ranji could not be swayed or stopped. He moved as a free man, unbound by role or duty, a ghost unshackled by the world's rules.

I could not chronicle his entire march; it sprawled too wide, twisted too deep. Often, I was too weary to lift my pen, my feet sore and my mind adrift. Yet the world took notice. Ranji flared into headlines, his wild journey sparking widespread interest. He was a force, a silent storm that refused to vanish.

His days had settled into rhythm, stark and simple. He woke before dawn, when the sky hung grey and the air brushed cool against his skin. He wore a cotton veshti knotted at his waist, a white shirt loose on his thinning frame, and walked barefoot, his soles toughened by endless miles. His possessions nestled in his shirt pocket: a fountain pen worn smooth, a pocket diary smudged with ink and a pair of scratched spectacles. A cotton bag held his spare veshti and a brick of soap; but he often forgot about the bag, leaving me to scramble after him with the small bundle. The angavastram over his shoulder doubled as towel and handkerchief, its edges frayed from use. He brushed his teeth with neem bark, snapping twigs from trees as he passed. Beyond this, Ranji carried nothing, a man stripped to the barest of essentials.

I was more than just a chronicler. I arranged security when the crowd swelled, found him privacy at night, coaxed food into him twice a day. He resisted like a child, turning away when not hungry, his eyes drifting elsewhere. A chapatti, a handful of rice, a sip of water; half would slip from his plate to a stray dog wagging its tail, a cow chewing in the shade, a monkey chattering above, or a crow perched on a wall.

'Eat, sir,' I would say, holding out a morsel. He would glance at me, his face blank, take a bite, then pass the rest to a creature nearby. I gave up arguing; it was his way, a quiet gift to the world he walked through.

He had no plans, no destination. Each morning he rose and moved, his path a riddle even to himself. He would leave national highways for state roads, then cut on to dusty tracks winding through fields. Village cartways came next, until he slid on to pathways threading between huts. Sometimes he traced abandoned railway tracks for miles, rusted rails stretching to nowhere, their ties choked with weeds. As dusk settled, he sought shelter: a school veranda with peeling paint, a temple courtyard ringing with bells or a mosque's cool expanse of stone. Gurdwaras welcomed him with langar, Jain temples offered a quiet corner, churches gave him a pew to rest. Any clean floor, any scrap of solitude, was enough.

Ranji sat, watching, listening to a stranger's pain, offering his hand to someone in need. But he never spoke, never waved, never let emotion crack his stillness. He ignored the cameras, the growing crowd, the shouts of his name. His detours were swift, leaving the swarm panting, lost in his dust. I began to see a thread in his chaos, a purpose in his aimless drift. He was guided not by maps but by an inner pull, a silent list of places erased from the world's gaze. This was an India beyond the spotlight, the real India of forgotten lives, and I became his shadow and his voice in this endless march.

In Kolkata, Ranji found a slum along the Hooghly river, a maze of tin roofs and muddy lanes. The air was heavy with coal smoke, the ground slick underfoot. Children darted past, barefoot and laughing; women cooked over flickering fires and elderly men sat idle, hands empty. Ranji walked in, his veshti streaked with dust, and stopped at a shack where a woman pounded rice. He pointed to a pile of broken bricks, a makeshift stove sputtering beside it.

The crowd surged. 'He is showing the city's shame!' a journalist shouted.

The woman, her sari threadbare, looked up. 'We build with scraps,' she said, her voice worn. 'No gas, no work, just this.'

Ranji's silence lifted her words, a cry from the margins. A volunteer, an older man named Sanjay, turned to me, his eyes glistening. 'He sees the invisible,' he said. 'I have lived here forever. No one else came.'

I nodded, scribbling, as Ranji moved on, the slum folding around him like a cloak.

In Gujarat, he reached a potters' colony near Bhuj, the air there thick with clay dust. Wheels spun under

ATULYA MISRA

skilled hands, shaping pots, lamps, idols—crafts woven into the earth's memory. Homes were mud, kilns smoked tirelessly, but the market had withered. Ranji stopped at a wheel, pointing to a stack of unsold wares, their glaze dulled.

A potter, his fingers crusted with clay, sighed. 'We make, but no one buys,' he said. 'Machines have taken our place.'

Ranji's gesture became a lament, a call for what was slipping away.

In Baramulla, cradled by the Jhelum beneath Himalayan peaks, a Silk Route legacy pulsed with endurance, yet power outages dimmed its dreams. A vendor in a weathered stall spoke to Ranji, his voice heavy. 'Empires crossed here, but darkness envelops our future.'

A student nearby added, 'No light, no study—how do we grow?'

Their words echoed the town's yearning for progress to match its grandeur.

In Chamba, the Ravi river's cadence sang of Himalayan serenity, yet flood-wrought ruins spoke of loss. A weaver by the debris-strewn banks told me, 'Our river gave life, but now it takes.'

A farmer added, 'Our fields drown and no help comes.'

Their plea unveiled a valley craving protection from calamity.

In Yadgir, Karnataka's Bhima river nurtured fields under Yadgir Fort's watchful gaze, but neglect marred its glory. A shopkeeper near littered slopes sighed. 'Kings built this, but we bury it in trash.'

A teenager muttered, 'Our history rots.'

Their shame reflected a struggle to reclaim their legacy.

In Visakhapatnam, where the Arabian Sea met epic lore atop sacred hills, pollution choked the tides. A fisherman by the shore said, 'Our gods unite here, but plastic kills our sea.'

A vendor added, 'We pray, but who cleans this?'

Their cry sought harmony with nature, a balance long broken.

In Vizianagaram, the fort's regal shadow crowned fertile plains, but jobless youth dimmed its pride.

A tailor by the moat said, 'Kings left wonders, but no work feeds us.'

A mother whispered, 'No doctors...our dreams dry up.'

Their voices unveiled a city yearning for progress to match its storied past.

Each conversation, vibrant against the backdrop of these enduring landscapes, framed Ranji's silent steps—a mirror to India's soul: resilient, scarred, yet ever hopeful.

A student, Neha, lingered beside me. 'He is like a mirror,' she said softly. 'Shows us what we forget.'

I looked at her, then at Ranji, his bare feet steady

on the ground. 'He is more,' I said. 'He is a memory we can't shake.'

In Bastar, Ranji ventured into Naxalite territory, where forests hid danger and villages bore scars. The air was tense, the trees thick with secrets. Central Reserve Police Force jawans tripled, their boots crunching, their voices sharp.

'Too risky,' one officer snapped into his radio. 'We cannot hold on to this situation.'

Ranji ignored them, walking a dirt path to a tribal hamlet. He stopped at a burnt-out hut, pointing to the charred remains.

A villager, his face hollow, said in a low voice, 'They came at night—Naxals, police, who knows? We are trapped in between.'

'He is showing war's cost!' a student cried.

Ranji's silence turned the ashes into a story, a wound laid bare.

A security man grabbed my arm. 'Tell him to go,' he said, eyes hard.

'I can't,' I replied. 'He does not hear. He never has.'

The officer cursed, then followed as Ranji slipped toward the forest's edge.

The world watched, caught in his grip.

'He is mad,' a journalist said once, wiping sweat from his face.

'No,' a volunteer replied, 'he is free.'

A student added, 'He is us—what we could be.'

Ranji walked on, silent, barefoot, a ghost with a purpose no one could pin down. He flagged poverty, craft, conflict—concerns buried in India's folds. The crowd swelled and faded, but he remained, a man without ties, a memory carved in dust. His march was endless, and I, his shadow, could only follow, whispering his silence to the world.

This is only a glimpse of Ranji's march—Kolkata's slums, Gujarat's fading pots, Bastar's charred homes. I cannot recount it all; his journey sprawled too wide, my pen too weary to follow every turn.

What follows in these pages are fragments of his travels—places plucked from the vast tapestry of his wanderings. They do not march in order or trace a path across the map. They are moments that caught my eye and stirred my heart—glimpses that echoed what Ranji seemed to seek, and what I, in some quiet way, recognized.

Part Two

Chapter 17

Where Guns Grew from Dust

We found ourselves in the Chambal ravines, a rugged expanse of muddy hillocks carved by restless rivers over centuries. The land stretched for hundreds of miles across Madhya Pradesh, Rajasthan and Uttar Pradesh, a maze of deep gullies and barren slopes. This was one of India's least developed regions, a place where progress seemed to stall. Caste conflicts simmered beneath the surface, opportunities were scarce and a gun culture lingered like a stubborn ghost. Above all, the Chambal was infamous for its dacoits, whose tales of notoriety and chivalry had woven themselves into the fabric of the land.

The ravines were a natural fortress, their twisting paths and steep drops making them the perfect hideout. For decades, dacoit gangs roamed here, their names echoing through villages: Man Singh, Roopa, Putli Bai,

Malkhan Singh... They were rebels to some, robbers to others, born from a mix of poverty, injustice and revenge. Vinoba Bhave, a Gandhian, had walked these same ravines, pleading for peace. He urged landlords to gift land to the tillers through the Bhoodan movement and convinced hardened dacoits to surrender. His voice, gentle yet firm, reached men like Mohar Singh, who laid down arms along with hundreds of others. Bhave's work offered a flicker of hope, a moment when the cycle of violence paused.

But the peace did not last. Poverty clung to the Chambal like dust, and unemployment gnawed at its people. Many who had surrendered drifted back into the ravines, picking up guns once more. Kidnapping, abduction, ransom and robbery became their occupation again. The terrain defied the police. Every footstep echoed; every move was watched from the hillocks. Gunfights erupted often, bullets tearing through the silence, claiming dacoits, policemen and innocent villagers caught in the crossfire. Bollywood turned these tales into blockbusters—*Mera Gaon Mera Desh*, *Sholay*, *Bandit Queen*, *Ganga Jamuna*—painting the Chambal as a land of outlaws and honour, a romanticized wilderness that hid its deeper wounds.

Ranji stepped into this world on a dusty afternoon. He wore his usual white shirt, which was now streaked with dirt. The highway cut through the ravines near Morena, and he veered off the asphalt, climbing a muddy hillock. The swarm followed—reporters with microphones, students with notebooks, security men with tense faces. I was there too, scribbling in my journal, watching him move with a purpose no one could name. He reached the top and stood still, gazing at the endless stretch of gullies below. The land looked wild and untamed, a sea of brown and green hiding secrets in its folds.

The crowd buzzed. 'What is he doing?' a young reporter asked, sweat beading on her forehead.

'Is he lost?' a student whispered, clutching his phone.

A policeman muttered into his radio, 'Keep the perimeter tight. This place is not safe.'

They were nervous, and for good reason. The ravines still whispered of danger. Though the famous bandits were gone, their shadows lingered. Some in the crowd turned back, haunted by the abduction tales they had heard as children. Ranji did not flinch. He fixed his gaze on the vastness below. No words, just a gesture—as if asking us to look at the ravines. See what had been forgotten.

The press scrambled for meaning. 'He's flagging neglect!' one shouted, camera rolling.

'Historic neglect of Chambal!' another typed furiously into her phone.

They were not wrong. The ravines were not just a hideout; they were a symptom. No roads reached deep into the villages, no schools stood firm, no jobs lifted the youth. Caste divided neighbours, and guns settled scores. Ranji's silent stand on that hillock woke the world to the consequences of leaving people behind. Headlines blared the next day: 'Former President Haunts Chambal, Exposes Decades of Apathy'.

From that hillock, Ranji descended and walked on, the swarm trailing him like a river. He reached Ambah, a small town in Morena district. Its streets were narrow and dusty. The air smelled of smoke and sweat, and children ran barefoot past crumbling houses. Ambah was a place of quiet struggle, its people tied to the land but starved of progress. Once, it had been a hotspot for dacoits, a recruiting ground for the desperate. Now, it was just poor—its fields patchy, its wells dry half the year.

The safety personnel grew edgy. 'Sir, we should move,' one said, scanning the horizon. 'This is not secure.'

Ranji ignored him, walking deeper into Ambah, past a temple with peeling paint, past a school with no roof. Each stop was a flag, a marker of broken promises. The press churned out stories: 'Ranji's Silent March Highlights Rural Decay'.

Students debated his intent, their voices rising. 'He is not political,' one argued; 'He is human,' another countered.

The crowd grew louder, but Ranji stayed quiet—a ghost among the living.

Next came Morena, a bigger town but no less

troubled. Its streets buzzed with rickshaws and vendors, poverty clinging to its edges. Ranji walked to the riverbank near Dholpur, the mud sucking at his feet. He stopped where the ravines met the water, a jagged line of earth torn open by time.

He stood still, the river glinting behind him, its surface hiding the depletion below. The headlines multiplied: 'Ghost President Exposes Chambal's Dying Rivers'.

Ranji's path carried him to Bhind, a district steeped in the gun culture of old. The ravines here had cradled dacoits like Malkhan Singh, who left behind a legacy of armed defiance. Bhind's people still carried guns, a habit born from necessity and pride—a matter of social status. Ranji walked its streets, past shops selling bullets alongside grain, past homes with barred windows. He stopped at a village square where a crowd of men sat smoking, their eyes wary. Ranji stared at a pile of rusted gun barrels stacked in a corner.

The crowd erupted. 'Gun culture!' a student yelled, filming the scene; 'He is showing the violence that won't die!' a reporter cried.

An old man, his beard white as cotton, approached. 'We kept guns to fight dacoits, then to fight each other,' he said, voice trembling. 'Now it is just habit. But it kills us still.'

Ranji's silence let the words sink in, a mirror held up to Bhind's past and present. The press seized it: 'Ranji's Ghost Walks Bhind, Flags Legacy of Arms'.

At Porsa, Ranji paused at a Dalit settlement, its huts small and frail. He pointed to a well, its rim chipped, its water reserved for upper castes. A woman in a faded sari watched him, her hands clasped. 'They will not let us near it', she said, her voice low. 'We walk miles for a bucket.'

The crowd hushed, then roared. 'Caste discrimination!' a student protested. 'He is exposing inequality!' a reporter typed.

Ranji moved on, his silence a thunderclap, and the headlines screamed: 'Ex-President's Silent Stand against Caste in Porsa'.

Finally, Ranji reached Gwalior, a city perched on the Chambal's edge, its fort looming over the plains. It was grander than the towns before, its streets wide, its history rich. Yet the ravines' shadow stretched here too—poverty and neglect seeping into its margins. Ranji walked to a slum near the railway tracks, where children played in dirt and mothers cooked over open fires. He stopped; his gaze fixed on a heap of garbage spilling into a ditch.

The swarm closed in. 'Urban neglect!' a reporter called. 'He's showing the city's underbelly!' a student added.

A boy, no older than ten, ran up, his shirt torn. 'No one cleans it', he said, kicking a plastic bottle. 'It stinks, and we get sick.'

Ranji's silence framed the boy's words, a spotlight on Gwalior's hidden rot. The press went wild: 'Ranji's Ghost Haunts Gwalior Slums, Flags Urban Decay'.

Ranji's journey was not merely a walk; it was a reckoning. He did not speak, did not need to. His gestures, his presence, flagged the real concerns—poverty, water, caste, guns and neglect. The crowd followed, growing with each step, their voices filling the void he left. Students debated his legacy, reporters chased his shadow, safety personnel fretted over his path. The world could not ignore Ranji. He was a walking ghost, a former president who had risen from obscurity to shine a light on the ignored.

Chapter 18

The Silence That Walked
Through Kashi

ashi, known to the world as Varanasi, greeted
Ranji with its timeless chaos. This was the abode
of Shiva as Mahakal, the great destroyer—a city
draped in myths of death and ultimate liberation. Yet
it throbbed with life, the oldest thriving urban sprawl
known to human civilization. Its narrow lanes twisted
like veins, its ghats hugged the Ganges, and its air
carried the weight of prayers and pyre smoke. People
came to Kashi to die, believing cremation on its ghats
would break the cycle of birth and rebirth forever.
Dharamshalas overflowed with the elderly, waiting
for their end, their eyes fixed on the river. Relatives
carried the dead through the *galis*—those tight, winding
streets—chanting '*Ram naam satya hai*, the name of
Rama is the truth', their cries piercing the din.

The ghats burned day and night. Pyres crackled at Manikarnika and Harishchandra, flames licking the sky as bodies turned to ash. The dead kept coming— an endless stream from across India, their families seeking salvation in the Ganges' embrace. Amid this theatre of mortality, life danced on. Men and women took holy dips in the river, their laughter mixing with the chants. Street vendors hawked jalebis dripping with syrup, kachoris stuffed with spice, and paanwallahs offered betel leaves, their red-stained smiles a Kashi signature. Bhang shops thrived, serving cannabis-laced drinks to locals and seekers alike, while grass smoke curled from quiet corners. Kashi belonged to everyone: pilgrims, tourists, sinners and saints—luring them with its galis (narrow streets), *gaali*s (abusive banter) and *goli*s (intoxicants).

Ranji stepped into this whirlwind on a humid morning. His white shirt hung loose, streaked with the dust of his travels. The swarm followed, a chaotic tail of cameras, microphones and nervous security men. He began at Dashashwamedh Ghat, the heart of Kashi's bustle, where priests chanted and bells rang. He stood at the water's edge, the Ganges lapping at his feet, and looked intently across the river. The crowd hushed, then buzzed.

'Pollution!' a student whispered, pointing at the greyish water flecked with debris. 'He's flagging the dying Ganges!' a reporter cried, snapping photos. A boatman nearby, his oar resting, spoke up. 'It is not merely the devotees and the cremations,' he said, his voice rough. 'Factories upstream dump everything. Fish are gone, and so is our living.'

Ranji's silence let the words echo, and the headlines roared: 'Ghost President Stands at Ganges, Exposes River's Plight'.

From Dashashwamedh, Ranji walked to Harishchandra Ghat, a quieter cremation site steeped in lore. The air here was thick with smoke, the scent of burning wood and flesh clinging to everything. Pyres glowed orange, tended by Doms, the keepers of the fire, who stacked logs with practised hands. Families wept, their faces shadowed by grief, while priests muttered mantras. Ranji stopped at a distance, his eyes fixed on the flames. He did not go too close, as if wary of his relationship with fire, a flicker of gratitude in his stillness. He looked towards a pile of unburnt logs beside a half-burnt pyre.

The swarm pressed in. 'There is a shortage of wood,' a traveller muttered, filming the scene. A Dom, his arms blackened with soot, stepped forward. 'We run out too fast,' he said, wiping sweat from his brow. 'Too many dead, not enough trees. Prices go up, and poor families can't pay.'

Ranji's silence framed the man's struggle, a spotlight on a hidden cost of death. The press seized it: 'Ranji's Ghost at Harishchandra, Flags Cremation Woes'.

Students whispered among themselves. 'He doesn't seem to be afraid of death,' one said. 'But he's showing its cost to the environment,' another replied.

We moved on to Manikarnika Ghat, Kashi's busiest cremation ground, where the fires never died. Like Harishchandra, this place too hummed with activity; pyres burned in rows, priests chanted, mourners carried bamboo biers through the crowd. Ranji stood on a stone ledge, the heat brushing his face, and moved towards a group of widows huddled in a corner, their heads shaved, their saris white. A woman, her voice frail, spoke to no one in particular. 'Custom takes away our hair, our colour, our lives,' she said, clutching a tattered shawl. 'No one cares after the fire.'

Ranji's gesture turned her words into a headline: 'Silent Ghost at Manikarnika Highlights Widows' Misery'.

He left the ghats and plunged into Kashi's galis, the narrow lanes pulsating with life. The streets were a labyrinth, barely wide enough for two to pass, lined with shops and homes stacked like cards. Here, the city's spirit thrived. Vendors shouted over one another, selling silk saris, brass idols and spicy chaat. Paan stains splattered the walls, and the air buzzed with curses and laughter. Ranji walked past a bhang shop, its counter crowded with men sipping green lassi. He stopped and moved towards a group of boys rolling hemp in a corner shop.

The crowd erupted. 'Drug abuse!' a student called, snapping a photo. 'He's flagging addiction!' a reporter typed furiously. A shopkeeper, his hands stained with betel nut, shrugged. 'It's Kashi,' he said. 'Bhang is as old as Lord Shiva here. But the kids take it too far—grass, pills, anything they find.'

Ranji's silence cut through the noise, and the headlines followed: 'Ghost President in Kashi Gali, Exposes Youth Addiction.'

Further into the lanes, he reached a weavers' quarter, where Muslim craftsmen wove Banarasi silk saris. The air hummed with the clack of looms, and small mosques called the faithful to prayer five times a day. Tiny outlets lined the gali, their floors cushioned with mattresses, no furniture in sight. Saris shimmered in piles—gold, red and green—displayed for buyers who sat cross-legged. Ranji paused at one such shop and took a weaver's hands in his own. They were cracked and calloused, working a threadbare loom.

The swarm leaned in. 'Exploitation!' a reporter shouted. 'He's showing the weavers' struggle!' a student added. The weaver, a thin man with tired eyes, looked up. 'We make beauty,' he said, his voice low. 'But we earn pennies. Middlemen take it all.' Ranji's gesture spoke for him, and the press ran with it: 'Ranji's Silent Stand in Kashi, Flags Weavers' Plight.'

A security man muttered, 'He's going too deep in here,' but Ranji pressed on, the gali swallowing him whole.

Ranji emerged from the lanes near the Kashi Vishwanath Temple, the beating heart of Hindu devotion. The golden spire gleamed in the sun as pilgrims thronged the courtyard, clutching jars of Ganges water to offer the Shivalingam. Temple architecture from every corner of India stood assembled in Kashi—Kerala's sloping roofs, Tamil Nadu's gopurams, Bengal's terracotta walls—each with priests chanting in regional tongues and serving food from their homelands.

Ranji moved past them, his eyes scanning the crowd, and stopped at a smaller shrine to Annapoorna, goddess of nourishment. He stood in a line of beggars, their bowls empty.

A priest, his forehead smeared with ash, sighed. 'We feed those we can,' he said. 'But they are too many, and the city forgets.' Ranji's silence turned the temple's wealth into a question, and the headlines blared: 'Ghost President at Kashi Vishwanath Temple, Finds Hunger at God's Door'.

He drifted to a small room nearby, a humble space where poet Subramania Bharati once lived in exile. The walls were cracked, the floor bare, but the air held the weight of his words—verses that fuelled India's fight for freedom. Ranji stood in the doorway, gazing emotionally at a faded photo of Bharati on the wall. The crowd hushed, then murmured. 'Legacy!' a student whispered. 'He is honouring the freedom fighters!' a reporter said. A local guide spoke up. 'Bharati wrote here, broke but free,' he said. 'His fire still burns in us.' The press captured it: 'Ranji's Ghost Visits Bharati's Room, Flags Forgotten Heroes'.

Next, he sought the home of Ustad Bismillah Khan, the shehnai maestro whose music once enchanted the world. The house was modest, tucked in a quiet lane, its windows dusty. Ranji stopped at the threshold; a broken shehnai rested on a shelf.

The crowd stirred. 'Culture fading!' a reporter shouted. 'He's showing art's neglect!' a girl added. An old woman with a wrinkled smile nodded. 'He played for Kashi, for India,' she said. 'Now his tunes are just memory.'

Ranji's gesture became a lament, and the headlines sang: 'Silent Ghost at Bismillah's Home, Flags Dying Music'.

Before the day waned, Ranji left Kashi's chaos for Sarnath, a few miles away, where the Buddha's teachings first took root. The air there was calmer, filled with chants and the rustle of prayer flags. Buddhist pilgrims from Japan, Sri Lanka, Vietnam, Cambodia and beyond gathered around the Dhamek Stupa, its stone weathered but proud. Built by Emperor Ashoka in the third century BC, this colossal structure marked the very spot where the Buddha delivered the Dhammacakkappavattana Sutta, his first teaching after Enlightenment.

Sarnath was Buddhism's cradle, a place of peace that drew the world to India's egalitarian soul. Here, centuries ago in the deer park of Isipatana, Gautama

Buddha delivered his first sermon, setting the Wheel of Dharma in motion. This was where Buddhism found its voice—where the noble truths were first spoken, where suffering was explained, and where the path to liberation was revealed.

As Ranji entered the sacred grounds, the air itself felt different, quieter, slower, as if infused with centuries of meditation. Buddhist monks in deep maroon and saffron robes walked in silence, their heads bowed, their movements unhurried. The rhythmic chants of sutras rose and fell like waves, their ancient syllables enveloping the space. Monks circumambulated the stupa in silent reverence, their hands clasped in prayer, rosary beads slipping through their fingers as they whispered ancient mantras. Some sat cross-legged under the shade of bodhi trees, their eyes half closed, meditating, lost in a realm beyond time.

Ranji, always the silent observer, stood at a distance, taking it all in. Unlike Kashi, where his mind was absorbed in the unending cycle of life and death, here he felt something different. A stillness. A vast emptiness that was not sorrowful, but deeply peaceful. It was as if the very land exhaled wisdom, inviting us to pause, to listen, to reflect.

Buddhism gave Indian civilization an egalitarian touch, something that resonated deeply with people from all walks of life. Unlike the rigid hierarchies of the time, the Buddha's teachings emphasized compassion over caste, wisdom over wealth, liberation over lineage.

It was this universal message that carried Buddhism far beyond India's borders. It spread eastward, taking root in China, Japan and Korea, shaping cultures, philosophies and even political systems. It wove itself into the fabric of Tibet, Sri Lanka, Myanmar and Thailand, where monks carried forward the teachings with unwavering devotion.

Ranji walked through the ruins of ancient monasteries, now reduced to red-brick foundations. He imagined what they must have looked like in their prime: scholars debating the finer nuances of the Tripitaka, monks chanting by the light of oil lamps and young novices sweeping the courtyards in the crisp morning air. Time had reclaimed these spaces, leaving only echoes behind.

He found himself standing before the Ashokan pillar, its smooth sandstone surface reflecting the midday sun. Once, it held the mighty Lion Capital, now preserved in a nearby museum, serving as the national emblem of India. The inscriptions on the pillar spoke of Ashoka's devotion to Dharma, his commitment to justice and non-violence—a king who turned away from war after witnessing its horrors.

For Ranji, this place was not merely an archaeological site. It was a mirror of time, a reminder that wisdom and compassion had always been stronger than swords and empires. For me, accompanying Ranji to Sarnath was more than a walk through history. It was a deeply personal experience, a connection to my own past.

As I moved through the sacred grounds, I thought of my father and grandfather, both of whom spoke of Sarnath with the reverence reserved for places that transcend time.

My grandfather, whom we called 'the Grambodha', was a man of stories. He narrated the Buddha's life with such vividness that it felt as if he had walked alongside him.

I could still hear his voice echoing in my mind, recounting how Siddhartha left his palace in search of truth, how he meditated under the bodhi tree in Bodh Gaya, and how he finally attained Enlightenment— not through divine intervention, but through sheer human effort. Standing in Sarnath, those stories came alive. Perhaps, in some way, we were all pilgrims—not necessarily in search of religious truths, but of meaning, understanding, something beyond ourselves.

Ranji's time in Kashi and Sarnath was not just a visit, it was a revelation. He flagged the Ganges' decay, the pyres' cost, the widows' grief, the youth's drift, the weavers' toil, the beggars' hunger, the past's fade and the present's promise—all without a word. The crowd gave voice to his silence, forming a chorus for the voiceless.

In one gali, a vendor told his friend, 'He sees what we live.'

At the ghats, a widow murmured, 'Maybe someone cares now.'

In Sarnath, a pilgrim smiled and said, 'He is quiet, like us.'

His journey became a mirror, reflecting Kashi's paradox: death and life, wealth and want, faith and neglect. The headlines piled up: 'Ranji's Ghost Haunts Kashi, Stirs Soul of Ancient City.'

The nation watched, unable to look away from the former president who walked as if death had freed him to see. As he left Sarnath, his wave carried on—a ghost unbound, a silent cry for India's forgotten corners.

Chapter 19

The Eyes That Did Not Look Away

Ranji, the barefoot former President, roamed India like a quiet storm, his mere presence peeling back layers of neglect. Lands long ignored, swept aside by media and the world, suffered in silence until his shadow loomed over them. He spoke no words, asked no questions, gave no replies. Yet his silent steps stirred the dust, spotlighting troubles buried deep.

His journey brought him to Manipur, a land of rolling hills, deep valleys and sprawling plateaus. The terrain twisted and turned, a patchwork of worn forests where shrubs and invasive plants had crept in. Dry paths snaked up steep slopes, bare rocks jutting out like the earth's bones. Yet water too flowed—across vast freshwater lakes glinting in the sun, floating swamps swaying gently, marshlands buzzing with species unique to this corner of the country. A place of stark beauty and deeper scars, Manipur had long been shaped by insurgency, martial law, border feuds, poverty and isolation. The people carried these marks in their eyes, their spirits tempered by a land both generous and harsh.

Manipur was a mosaic of ethnic groups: headhunting Nagas, steadfast Kukis, mainstream Meiteis, and countless smaller groups, each with their own voice and way of life. For centuries, they lived woven together, peace held by a fragile thread. The women were striking, their beauty a quiet force, while the men were tough, carved by the rugged hills. Sport flowed in their blood— boxing, native polo, wrestling, Thang Ta, martial arts, football—all reflecting their instinct for resilience and action. This was a land where strength ran deep, and the past lingered in every ridge and stream.

From the highlands they came—tribals pouring into Imphal, the valley town cradling most of Manipur's heartbeat. A near-stampede broke out, voices shouting, hands waving, as they glimpsed the walking saint. Imphal's streets buzzed with shops selling woven shawls, stalls frying fish and children darting through the fray. Ranji slipped into a Sanamahi temple, its steps steep, its gods human-like, perched on pedestals in layered rooms. Snakes coiled at their bases, a nod to the Meitei belief that ancestors slithered from another realm.

Girls wore embroidered skirts over flowing dresses,

their hands swift with needle and thread. Children grinned and fidgeted, too restless to sit, while old men gazed into the distance, a blissful calm on their faces. Older women, keepers of songs and rituals, watched him pass, their eyes rich with memory.

Manipur's story stretched back centuries, a kingdom fierce and proud. Once an independent realm, it was ruled by Meitei kings who traced their lineage to ancient gods. These kings governed from Kangla, their legacy etched into the land. In the eighteenth century, rulers like Garib Nawaz brought Vaishnavism to the Meiteis, blending it with Sanamahi beliefs; centuries earlier, King Kyamba had traded with Shan kings and gifted polo to the world. Their palaces, now crumbling ruins or restored relics, stood as echoes of lost power.

In the nineteenth century, the British arrived, their boots trampling the land's sovereignty after the Anglo-Manipur war of 1891. The royal flag fell, but the spirit endured, flaring again when Netaji Subhas Chandra Bose chose Manipur as a base in the fight for India's freedom. During the Second World War, the hills turned into battlegrounds, as Japanese and Allied forces clashed near Imphal and Kohima, leaving behind graves and tales. After 1947, Manipur merged with India, but the union was uneasy; demands for autonomy flared into insurgency. Its isolation, tucked in the Northeast, kept it distant, its struggles muted by the noise of the mainland.

Ranji walked past a faded royal banner in Imphal,

his fingers grazing its frayed edge. An old man, his eyes distant, remarked, 'They ruled us once. Now they are merely stories.'

Ranji's silence honoured the end of their reign.

Imphal's palace, Kangla Fort, rose from the city's heart, a relic of Meitei pride. Its walls, once made of mud and brick, had stood firm through centuries, protecting a moat and sprawling grounds. Temples dotted its expanse, their roofs curved, their gods ancient—Pakhangba, the dragon lord, watching over all. The British seized the fort, then left; now it stood open, a bridge between past and present.

Ranji walked its paths, pausing at a cracked pillar, its base worn by time.

'Neglect!' a volunteer called out. 'He is flagging faded glory!' a journalist cried. An old caretaker, his hands folded, said, 'This was our pride. Now it waits—like us—helplessly, for someone to restore it.'

Ranji's silence turned the fort into a memory, a quiet call to what once was.

From there he travelled to Keibul Lamjao, a wonder of nature cradled by hills. The world's only floating national park, it drifted on phumdis—thick mats of vegetation afloat on Loktak Lake. Loktak itself was a vast mirror reflecting the sky, its banks fringed with reeds and lotus. Fishermen glided in dugout canoes, their nets slicing through the surface; herons and kingfishers danced above, as if painting the air.

But the lake was shrinking, choked by silt from deforested hills, invaded by weeds and human hands. Ranji stood on its shore, pointing to the receding waterline, his silence a call to the beauty slipping away.

The Sangai deer moved across the phumdis, a creature of grace found nowhere else. Its antlers curved like slender branches, its coat a soft brown, its hooves adapted for floating land. Known as the dancing deer, it moved with delicate poise, in harmony with the lake's rhythm, indifferent to man or beast. Hunted to near extinction, it clung to survival, a symbol of Manipur's fragile wild.

Ranji raised his hand as one emerged from the swamp, head high, eyes calm.

The crowd gasped. 'Endangered!' a student cried. 'He is showing what we are losing!' a journalist shouted. A park guide said softly, 'There are few left. The lake is their life; if it goes, they go.'

Ranji's gesture held the deer's fate, a quiet plea for its world.

He walked on to Moreh, a border town brushing Myanmar, where the Tamil community had made its home for over a century. Neat rows of graves lined the town's edge, markers of young lives lost to wars and clashes—some from distant battles, others from local strife.

Ranji stood among them, pointing to the weathered stones.

The crowd gathered behind him. 'Forgotten dead!' a student called, scribbling fast. 'He is showing the cost of conflict!' a journalist shouted, camera clicking. A Tamil elder said quietly, 'They fought for something, but we are left with graves.'

Ranji's gesture turned the silent graves into a tale, a muted cry for those buried and unseen.

From there, he drifted past houses abandoned in ethnic clashes—their walls blackened, their roofs caved in. He pointed. The crowd murmured. 'Displacement!' cried a volunteer. 'He is flagging lost homes!' added a journalist. A woman in a patched sari stepped forward. 'We ran when the fighting came,' she said. 'Now there is nothing to return to.'

Ranji moved on, his silence a mirror to her loss.

He passed burnt poppy fields, their ashes stark against the green foliage, and floating villages on Loktak Lake—huts on stilts that once hid Indian National Army soldiers. At the Myanmar border, his toes grazed the line, but he turned back at the last moment, as if tugged by an unseen force.

Manipur unfolded before him, a land of beauty and pain, strength and neglect. He walked its hills, its valleys, its swamps—flagging truths buried in silence: insurgency's grip, ethnic wounds, vanishing water, poppy's curse, a lake's slow death.

The crowd followed, their voices filling his silence. 'He is waking us,' a volunteer told me, her eyes bright.

'To what we have ignored,' I replied, my pen racing.

A security man grumbled, 'He is trouble; goes where we cannot guard.'

I shrugged. 'He is free,' I said. 'That is his shield.'

Ranji's march through Manipur was just one thread in his vast weave, a glimpse of a journey that stretched far beyond my grasp. There is more to tell, more lands he graced with his silence, waiting to be unfolded.

Chapter 20

The Barefoot Saint in Sikkim

After wandering through the seven sister states of the Northeast—Assam, Meghalaya, Manipur, Tripura, Nagaland, Arunachal Pradesh and Mizoram—Ranji turned towards Sikkim. A light shawl draped his thin frame, shielding him from the chill that drifted down from the mountains. Behind him stretched a sea of people: volunteers drawn by his quiet pull, security men with watchful eyes, journalists hungry for stories, students scribbling in notebooks and onlookers caught in his spell. The crowd swelled, nearly choking the narrow roads, their voices a hum against the silence he carried.

We were crossing the chicken neck of India—a slender strip of land cradling Siliguri, squeezed between Bangladesh, Nepal, Tibet and Myanmar. This fragile corridor tethered the Northeast and

Sikkim to the rest of the country, a lifeline pulsing with complexity. International borders pressed closely, turning domestic troubles into knots of human rights. The landscape unfolded in layers: tea gardens sprawled across gentle slopes, the tea leaves deep green under the sun; degraded forests stood sparse and weary; marshlands shimmered with hidden life; and patches of lush semi-deciduous woods burst with colour, sheltering elephants and offering fleeting glimpses of wildlife. The air carried the scent of damp earth and distant snow, a reminder of the mountains looming ahead.

This was a land of unrest and resilience. Terrorist groups flickered in the shadows, their presence a low rumble alongside the fading red corridor of Naxalite echoes. Migrant labourers and refugees poured in, their footsteps adding to the region's tangled weave. Occupations shifted like the wind—farmers turned tea pluckers, traders became smugglers—while borders redrew themselves through history's churn. People adapted, their ways bending under waves of change; towns swelled into administrative hubs, military bases sprouted, hydroelectric dams rose, strategic roads cut through the earth, and tourism bloomed with its promise of escape.

Ranji walked through it all—his bare feet pressing the soil, his silence louder than the chaos—clad in a white shirt, veshti knotted at the waist, an angavastram draped over his shoulder and a woollen shawl to brace against the cold.

Our path from Siliguri to Gangtok climbed steadily, and the world shifted around us. Vegetation thickened and then thinned, giving way to pine and rhododendron. Human settlements studded the slopes, their tin roofs glinting and prayer flags fluttering; culture morphed with every mile. Bengali chatter faded into Nepali songs, Lepcha greetings and Bhutia calls. The Teesta river flowed beside us, its waters a restless green thread slicing through the valleys and feeding the land. Ranji's shawl fluttered in the breeze, his steps slow but sure, the crowd trailing behind, their breath fogging in the cooling air.

I exhaled in relief when Ranji did not detour towards Bhutan. Instead, we pressed on to Gangtok, bustling with shops and stupas, its air crisp with the smell of pine. A crowd clogged the roads here too, their murmur a constant companion.

Ranji paused at a chorten and glanced at a pile of faded prayer flags flapping in the wind. 'He is showing forgotten faith!' a student called, camera clicking. A monk in his saffron robes said, 'These were offerings once. Now they fray.'

Ranji's silence turned the flags into a story, a call to honour what time had worn thin.

Sikkim unfolded like a world apart, a Buddhist kingdom once ruled by Lepcha kings, its history steeped in mountain mist. Long ago, its domain stretched across Kalimpong, Darjeeling, parts of Bhutan and swathes of Nepal. The Chogyals, its monarchs, ruled from Gangtok, their palace a fortress of wood and stone perched on a ridge. Wars with Nepal and Bhutan left lasting scars, shrinking its borders until the British made it a protectorate in the nineteenth century. Treaties bound Sikkim to colonial whims, keeping its kings in check while the mountains stood guard. After 1947, India inherited this arrangement—a quiet pact that held until 1975.

That year, whispers of conspiracy spread—secret meetings, espionage and a king caught in a web. Palden Thondup Namgyal, the last Chogyal, faced mounting demands for democracy. Under pressure, he invited India to intervene. The monarchy dissolved, Sikkim became the twenty-second Indian state, and the army solidified its hold over the fragile northeastern flank.

Yet the intrigue lingered like mist on the ridges. Namgyal's American wife, Hope Cooke, left for the United States after his fall, her life darkened by the deaths of their two sons—one to cancer, the other to a car crash. The palace in Gangtok remained a private shell for survivors, its walls heavy with secrets.

Even as history settled into stone, Sikkim's spiritual heart beat strong. Monasteries like Rumtek and Enchey rose from the hills, their golden roofs gleaming, prayer wheels spinning tales of devotion. These sanctuaries nestled in quiet valleys where monks chanted and butter lamps flickered, echoing ancient rhythms. Sikkim stood a pocket of peace, its serenity guarded by army posts, its trails alive with tourists chasing glacial lakes, high deserts, Himalayan peaks, and the quiet thrill of staring across tense borders at uneasy neighbours.

But beneath the calm, geopolitics stirred. China loomed to the north, casting a long shadow over Nathu La, the high mountain pass where Indian and Chinese soldiers stood eye to eye across barbed wire. Ranji paused near the pass, before a rusted bunker half-buried in snow.

A soldier, breath fogging in the cold, said, 'We watch day and night. Peace is thin.'

Ranji's silence turned the bunker into a sentinel, a symbol of a land always on edge.

Sikkim's culture shone through its people. Lepchas, the original dwellers, spoke soft and slow, weaving tales of spirits in forests and rivers. Bhutias, traders from Tibet, carried the quiet of Buddhism, their prayer beads clicking in rhythm with the hills. Nepalis, now the largest group, filled the slopes with Gorkha songs and dances, their khukuris gleaming at their waists. Festivals lit the calendar: Losar welcomed the Tibetan New Year with masked dances and momo feasts; Saga Dawa honoured the Buddha with processions to hilltop monasteries; Pang Lhabsol paid tribute to Mount Kanchenjunga, the guardian peak, with chants and offerings.

　　　　ATULYA MISRA

A Bhutia elder, his voice gravelly, told us, 'We dance, but our young are leaving.'

Ranji's silence turned the dance into memory, a fading echo of tradition drifting away.

From Gangtok, he veered northward, into terrain wilder and more remote. The state required Inner Line Permits here—a barrier that thinned the crowd. Journalists and casual travellers stayed behind, idling in Gangtok's comfort while the rest of us pressed on. North Sikkim was a trial: thick forests of fir and bamboo, jagged and steep roads scarred by landslides, villages sparse and scattered. The Teesta river roared below, its waters fed by countless waterfalls tumbling from high ridges.

The flora dazzled—orchids in brilliant bloom, ferns unfurling over damp stones. The fauna shifted too: monkeys and langurs gave way to thickset livestock, then to yaks as we climbed. Plump, woolly dogs wagged their tails, more charming than any bred pet. Houses grew scarce, their sloped wooden roofs clinging to cliff edges, chimneys trailing smoke into the thin air.

In Lachung, a village cradled by mountains, Ranji stopped beside a stream choked with silt. A villager, his face creased and brown as bark, said, 'The rains wash everything down. Our fields shrink.'

Ranji's silence framed the stream's struggle—a quiet plea for soil slipping away. The crowd had thinned, but its voice remained clear in the rarefied air.

North Sikkim stunned. The Yumthang Valley bloomed with rhododendrons, a vibrant carpet of red and pink spread across snow-fringed meadows. Gurudongmar Lake shimmered at 17,000 feet, turquoise and sacred, its shores kissed by icy winds. Kanchenjunga towered above, its peaks a god to the Sikkimese and a challenge to climbers.

A herder, standing with his yak, said, 'The snow thins each year. Our pasture shrinks.'

Ranji's silence turned the ice into a warning, a silent cry for a world warming too fast.

Through each step, Sikkim unfolded as a land of peace and peril, beauty and burden. Ranji moved through it—over slopes, into valleys, across passes— flagging what lay buried in silence: the quiet erosion of monarchy, the tensions at the border, the slow scarring of nature, the fraying of tradition. His presence made these absences visible.

The crowd followed, some whispering, some wide-eyed.

'He is waking us,' said a volunteer beside me, her eyes bright.

'To what we missed,' I replied, my pen trembling.

A security man muttered behind us, 'He is trouble, going where we cannot follow.'

'That is his path,' I replied, my breath short.

Volunteers huddled close, their voices softer now,

while students scribbled with numb fingers. Ranji pointed at a gash of mud and rocks across a ridge. A villager, her shawl tight, said, 'The landslide took our road last rains. We are cut off.'

Ranji's silence turned the scar into a story, a mark of a land unsteady.

Chapter 21

A City of Shadows and Shine

R anji's wandering feet had carried him across the vastness of India, from dusty villages to bustling towns, through forests and plains, until they finally brought him to Mumbai. The city rose before him like a living beast, its pulse throbbing with energy, its breath a mix of sweat, sea breeze and smoke. He chose Dharavi, the largest slum in India, as his base. Dharavi was a sprawling maze of narrow lanes and tin roofs, a place where the voices of local Marathis mingled with Tamil, Telugu, Bhojpuri and countless other tongues, weaving a dense symphony of survival.

Here, poverty clung to every corner, hygiene was a distant dream, crime lurked in the shadows and civic amenities were scarce. Yet amidst the chaos, there was a strange strength—a social capital that bound people together. Loneliness had no place here: the air buzzed with chatter, laughter and the clatter of daily life. Every household doubled as a workshop, a tiny engine of commerce. Hands worked tirelessly—stitching clothes, hammering metal, shaping goods—each pair contributing to a chaotic web of economic activity. Wages were small, piece rates smaller still, but they fuelled a cycle of dependence for the workers and profit for the middlemen who thrived above them. There were no neat chains of production, no clear paths forward or back, merely a wild dance of effort and skill, hemmed in by geography, limited resources and a chronic lack of capital. Dharavi was like a directionless, shapeshifting amoeba, always moving, always adapting, yet stationary all the same.

To rise in Dharavi, one had to become something more—a leader, a politician, a saviour, a miracle worker. The youth carved their own escapes: their energy spilled into gully cricket matches where a worn ball bounced off crumbling walls, or street dances that turned dusty alleys into stages. Some flexed their muscles in makeshift gyms, others clashed in fleeting street fights, and a few chased nothing at all, running aimlessly until exhaustion brought them to a stop. Women, meanwhile, found solace in faith. Street corners held tiny idols and miniature temples, always crowded with poor women offering flowers or coins from their meagre earnings, their prayers rising above the din. Beggars lingered nearby, hands outstretched, some quietly pocketing more in a day than the people who gave them charity. Life here was a grind, a relentless push against odds stacked high.

With a bit of direction, a sprinkle of planning, a touch of care, Dharavi might have leapt forward. But the answers would not come from grand schemes or towering blueprints. They needed to be small, specific, woven into the fabric of each life. The planning had to take the shape of micro-plans, micro-investments, and micro-solutions for Dharavi's mega problems. The intellectuals, the investment bankers, the dreamers with their redevelopment models and capital-heavy fixes could not crack this place. Dharavi was too tangled, too alive, its function in the megacity too deep-rooted for outsiders to grasp.

Ranji settled into a Tamil household, sleeping soundly on a thin mat, the familiar smells of idli and soaked rice wafting through the air. He used the community toilets without complaint, ate with his hands and watched the world unfold around him.

Mumbai was a city of two faces, and Ranji felt them both as he wandered its streets. On one side it gleamed with economic might, a powerhouse fuelling the nation's wealth. Towers of glass and steel pierced the sky, their windows catching the sun like shards of mirror. The stock exchange hummed with frantic trades, brokers shouting into phones, fortunes rising and falling with each tick of the clock. Banks lined the roads, their marble façades exuding calm, while factories churned out goods shipped across the globe. The film industry glittered nearby, a dream machine spinning tales of love and valour, its stars strutting through studios and premieres, their faces plastered on billboards looming above the city.

This was the Mumbai of prosperity, a magnet for ambition, a place where history whispered of trade and conquest. Portuguese ships had docked here centuries ago, followed by Dutch and British merchants who turned a cluster of islands into a colonial jewel. The Gateway of India still stood as a relic of that past, its arches gazing out at the sea, a silent witness to the city's rise.

Yet on the other side sprawled the slums, where millions lived in the shadow of that wealth. Shanties leaned against each other, patched with tarpaulin and plastic, their roofs sagging under monsoon rains. Narrow lanes twisted like veins, choked with people, handcarts and the occasional stray dog. Here, the air smelled of sweat and sewage—not sea breeze and success. Children played barefoot in puddles, their laughter mingling with the clatter of pots and the cries of vendors. For every glistening skyscraper, there was a slum stretching wide—a reminder that Mumbai's prosperity was not universal. Ranji walked these streets, his eyes tracing the divide.

He saw the dabbawallahs, those quiet heroes of the

city, weaving through the chaos with their tiffin boxes. Clad in white kurtas and caps, they carried meals from homes to offices with clockwork precision, a tradition born decades ago as workers and office-goers needed their lunches delivered from home. Each box was a thread in Mumbai's fabric, a link between domestic life and the economy, a marvel of coordination in a city that often defied order.

The suburban trains were another lifeline, their metal bodies rattling across tracks that stitched the city together. Ranji rode them once, pressed shoulder to shoulder with commuters, the air thick with heat and human breath. Carriages groaned under the weight of bodies, doors hanging open as men clung to the edges, their faces grim with determination. These trains carried Mumbai's soul, ferrying millions each day—clerks, labourers, students, dreamers—all bound for work and some vague notion of destiny. Stations pulsed with life, platforms bursting with hawkers selling tea and vada pav, the scent of spices slicing through diesel fumes. This was Mumbai's heartbeat—relentless, raw and real.

The film industry caught Ranji's attention, though he kept his distance. He passed studios where lights blazed and cameras rolled, where actors rehearsed lines and dancers swayed to unheard beats. The city thrived on these stories, its people flocking to theatres to escape their struggles, if only for a few hours. This was another Mumbai—a city of celluloid dreams and glittering illusions, where glamour floated above grit.

I sometimes wondered what his life might have been had he chased such a path. The thought first brought a smile and then loud laughter.

One evening, he sat by the sea at Marine Drive, the waves lapping gently against the stones. The necklace of lights curved along the shoreline, a sight that had once welcomed kings and conquerors. I found the city alive. Too alive. It gives and takes, lifts and crushes. I saw myself in its shadows, but not its shine. Mumbai was a mirror, reflecting India's triumphs and trials, its history of resilience and its present of struggle. We all felt small beside it, and yet somehow part of it, like wanderers caught in its tide.

But as the days wore on, restlessness crept in—not just for Ranji, but for those who travelled with him. The perpetual stench, the unending noise, the constant press of bodies began to wear them down. Living in slums was not for everyone. Security personnel, media folk and other co-travellers who had joined the former President began to murmur. There was too much to take in, too much raw life pressing in at every turn.

As Ranji prepared to leave, Mumbai's contradictions stayed with us. The economic powerhouse roared on, its wealth a beacon to the world, while the slums sprawled in its shadow, a testament to its blind spots. The trains still rumbled, the dabbawallahs pedalled on, the film reels spun, and Ranji, the former President, walked through it all—silent and steady. Mumbai had shown its soul. We carried it with us as we moved onward, the Western Ghats rising in the distance, and Goa waiting just beyond.

Chapter 22

Beaches, Bells and Broken Promises

Ranji stepped on to the warm sands of Goa, his bare feet sinking into the grains as the salty breeze brushed his face. The sun hung low in the sky, casting a golden glow over the endless coastline. He had wandered across India—from the towering mountains of the north to the bustling cities of the south—but Goa felt different. It buzzed with a strange energy, a mix of serenity and chaos, history and excess, all woven into the fabric of its beaches, churches, and swaying coconut palms. Once shaped by Portuguese rule, Goa still bore traces of its colonial past in its architecture, its food, and its people. The Portuguese left behind their churches with weathered white walls, spicy vindaloo, and a passion for football that echoed through the villages. Even after India reclaimed it—first as a Union Territory, then as a state—Goa held on to its singular essence.

Ranji found a small fishing hamlet to call home for a while. The fishermen greeted him with quiet nods, their hands busy untangling nets as boats bobbed in the shallows. Their lives revolved around the sea, a rhythm unbroken for generations. Ranji, a former president now wandering in silence, felt an unexpected peace. Their simplicity—casting nets at dawn, returning with the catch by noon, sipping feni under the stars—stood in sharp contrast to the madness we would soon uncover beyond the hamlet.

Walking barefoot along the shore, I watched the waves crash gently, their foam kissing his toes. The beaches stretched for miles, some serene and untouched, others teeming with life. Goa had become India's leisure hub, a place where the world came to escape. Luxury resorts with infinity pools and swaying hammocks lined the coast, their neon signs promising paradise. Shacks dotted the sands, serving cold beer and fiery prawn curry, the owners calling out to tourists with wide grins. However, beneath the postcard beauty, something darker simmered.

Ranji wandered north, past the shacks and into beaches where trance music throbbed through the air. The scene shifted. Packs of young travellers from Europe, Russia, and Israel wandered sunburned and laughing. Many were on shoestring budgets, chasing freedom, drugs, and the vestiges of the hippie trail. Clothes were optional. On some hidden shores, bodies lay sprawled under the sun, unconcerned by curious stares. I heard a fisherman mutter, 'They think this is theirs now,' his voice low and resigned.

The foreigners carved out enclaves of their own. Russians dominated one stretch, Cyrillic signs marking their bars, techno beats pounding into the night. Israelis gathered nearby, their chatter in Hebrew, their rhythms distinct. Smack parties, as the locals called them, raged after dark. Drugs flowed freely—ganja, ecstasy, and harder substances trafficked by shadowy figures. Ranji saw it all, unnoticed, a silent observer among the revellers. The irony was striking—this quiet fishing haven now drowning in its own allure, its beauty commodified and corroded.

Yet history still lingered. The churches stood like sentinels, their bells cutting through the din. Ranji stepped into one, pressing his palms against its cool stone. A priest approached, his robes trailing. 'This was Portugal's heart,' he said softly. 'They built us, shaped us. Now we're something else.'

Ranji nodded, feeling the weight of years—Portuguese rule, Indian liberation, and now this tourist invasion—stacked like layers of bebinca.

We met Antony one evening, a wiry Goan with salt-and-pepper hair, sipping port wine outside his shack. 'This isn't the Goa I knew,' he said, eyes on the horizon.

'We used to fish, pray, play football on Sundays. Now? It's all noise and plastic.' He gestured at a pile of bottles and wrappers strewn across the sand. 'Tourists come, and this is what they leave behind. And the mining... Have a look at the hills.'

Ranji followed his gaze inland, where the green slopes bore ugly red scars from iron ore mines. The earth had been torn open, rivers choked with silt, all for profit that rarely reached the fishermen and farmers.

Antony took a sip of his wine. 'The church still holds us together, you know. On Sundays we still sing the old hymns. But even that's fading. The young ones want clubs and cocktails.'

Ranji nodded. The Portuguese had left their marks—crosses atop whitewashed chapels gleaming in the sun. But the new gods were money and tourism.

Still, some traditions endured. One afternoon, Ranji came across a dusty field where boys chased a football with fierce joy. Their shouts echoed as they darted barefoot across the earth. 'It's in our blood,' said a local named Mickle, wiping sweat from his brow. 'The Portuguese gave us this. We don't need much—just a ball and a patch of ground.'

Ranji smiled. Amid the chaos, this felt true, a thread that still held.

However, not all threads were so innocent. As he moved deeper into the underbelly of Goa, darker whispers followed. Paedophiles, drawn by lawlessness and anonymity, lurked in the shadows. There were rumours of missing children, their families too poor or frightened to resist. Neo-hippies preached peace and love, their dreadlocks swinging as they strummed guitars, but some hid sinister appetites. The police often turned a blind eye, greased by bribes from the mafia that ran the drug cartel. Illegal construction boomed along the coast. Buildings sprouted like weeds, flouting every coastal regulation. Towers of concrete loomed over the beaches, their foundations sinking into the sand.

'They call it progress,' a woman named Lilly told Ranji one day, her voice sharp as she sold petrol in old whisky bottles by the roadside. 'But it is killing us. The fish do not come like they used to. The water is dirty.' She pointed to a nearby river, its surface slick with oil from the mines upstream.

Arjun, one of our co-travellers, bought a bottle from her, the sharp smell of fuel mixing with the sea air, a strange symbol of Goa's contradictions.

The food, though, was a revelation. One evening, I joined Arjun at a shack. The owner piled our plates with fish recheado, stuffed with fiery red masala and served with fluffy sannas—steamed rice cakes from the Portuguese playbook. A glass of feni sat beside it, its musky bite cutting through the spice. Later, we also tried bebinca, a layered dessert rich with coconut and jaggery, its sweetness lingering on his tongue. The cuisine was Goa itself: bold, mixed, a dance of cultures.

Yet even this was changing; tourists demanded burgers and pizzas, and the shacks obliged.

Another night, I left Ranji in peace and, along with some young volunteers, slipped into a pub, its wooden walls shaking with bass. Locals and foreigners mingled, their glasses filled with feni, the cashew liquor that burned going down. A Russian named Sasha stumbled over, his eyes glassy. 'This place is magic,' he slurred, spilling his drink. 'No rules, only freedom.' I watched as Sasha swayed back into the crowd. Freedom, yes. Freedom at what cost?

The thrill of Goa was undeniable. The beaches glowed under moonlight, the waves an endless lullaby. The parties thrummed with life, their energy infectious. Ranji probably felt it too, the pull of this wild, untamed land. But the issues gnawed at him. The fishermen struggled, their boats dwarfed by cruise liners. The mines poisoned land and water. Drugs hollowed out young lives. Garbage climbed higher. Locals were trapped—trying to preserve home while profiting from its slow decay.

He met an environmentalist one morning, her hands stained with soil from a protest site. 'We are losing Goa,' she said, her voice trembling. 'The mines, the buildings, the trash—it is too much. And the government? They do not care. They see dollars, not destruction.' She showed him photos of a beach before and after: once pristine, now a mess of bottles and concrete.

Ranji listened, his silence a comfort to her. His presence, a former president walking barefoot among protestors, drew eyes. Soon, journalists arrived, their cameras flashing, their questions sharp. Reports and documentaries of Goa's struggles—pollution, drugs, coastal decay—spread, a flicker of hope amid the chaos.

One evening, as the sun dipped below the waves, Ranji sat with Mickle again. The football game had ended, the boys laughing as they ran home. 'You see it all, do you not?' Mickle asked, his eyes searching Ranji's face. 'The good, the bad. What do you think?'

Ranji paused, then wrote on the sand: 'It is a beautiful mess.'

Mickle chuckled, nodding. 'That is Goa.'

Goa was a land of serene beaches and secret sins, of memory and mayhem. The past whispered through the coconut palms, the present roared from speakers at night. Ranji stayed longer than he'd planned, drawn by its ache and its beauty. This wasn't just a stop—it was a mirror, reflecting the wild, wounded heart of the nation, and the cost of its dreams.

Chapter 23

The Silent Steps to Bodh Gaya

Ranji's journey across India took him to the dusty plains of Bihar, his bare feet now tracing the sacred paths of Gaya. He had walked across mountains and rivers, through cities alive with noise and villages wrapped in quiet, but Bodh Gaya felt like a pull from deep within. This was no ordinary town. It was the cradle of Buddhism, a place where a prince named Siddhartha Gautama became the Buddha under a bodhi tree, his mind unlocking the secrets of life more than two and a half millennia ago. Ranji, the former president who had stepped away from power to wander in silence, now approached this holy ground, a calm presence amid the crowd trailing him.

We walked alongside him, our steps keeping pace, though none could match his stillness. People always hovered nearby—media with clicking cameras, curious locals, travellers drawn by his legend—but Ranji remained quiet, his eyes absorbing everything. The road from Patna to Gaya stretched long and dry, flanked by fields and slow carts pulled by bony oxen. Bodh Gaya shimmered in the distance like a promise.

When we finally arrived, the air changed. It carried the faint scent of incense and the murmur of chants, a softness that settled over us.

We stopped beneath the bodhi tree, its wide branches casting dappled shade. This was no ordinary tree—it was a descendant of the one Siddhartha had once sat under, its heart-shaped leaves trembling in the breeze. Mats lay scattered around, people meditating in silence, their breaths slow and deep. Ranji lowered himself on to one, crossed his legs, and closed his eyes. He had walked away from his own funeral pyre, moved through India's chaos, but never before had we seen him like this—so still, so completely at peace. A woman in our group nudged me. 'Look at him,' she whispered. 'He is different here.'

'Do not bother him,' I murmured, my voice low but firm. The media folks, their cameras hanging unused for once, nodded in agreement. Ranji's calm was a thread binding us together, and we let him be, turning to explore the sacred grounds.

The complex hummed with life yet held a stillness that sank into our bones. Beneath the tree, the Vajrasana gleamed—a sandstone slab etched with goose and palmette designs, marking the spot where the Buddha attained Enlightenment. Above it, a gilded statue glowed, its golden face serene.

At the heart of it all stood the Mahabodhi Temple, its spire slicing into the sky. The temple's brick and stucco walls were carved with figures of the Buddha, his hands raised in blessing, his expression calm. Monks in saffron robes glided past, prayer beads in hand. Pilgrims from Japan, Thailand and Sri Lanka knelt beside one another, each face turned inward. Ranji entered the temple alone, his bare feet steady on the warm stone. The crowd parted around him like water around a rock.

We moved closer, our fingers brushing the cool stone. 'This place feels alive,' Neha said, tracing a niche.

A local man overheard her; 'It has been here forever,' he said, nodding. 'The Buddha sat, thought, changed everything. You feel it, don't you?'

Neha nodded, and he smiled, walking off with a basket of flowers swinging in his hands.

We explored the complex, our hands on the Vajrasana's smooth surface, our eyes tracing the temple's carvings. The sacred ground held us, its stillness a mirror for our questions. For Ranji, it was a brief pause, a moment of peace in his endless journey. For us, it was a chance to breathe, to feel the weight of something greater.

The past was everywhere. Pilgrims chanted, their voices audible over the rustle of leaves. Tourists snapped photos, their laughter a faint ripple against the reverence. The air shimmered with meaning, pulling us into its embrace. For a moment, the world's noise—its fights, its greed—slipped away, replaced by a simplicity that tugged at our hearts. Here, life wasn't about ambition or power. It was about letting go. Understanding. Finding something deeper.

Beyond the temple, Bodh Gaya unfolded in layers. Vendors lined the streets, their stalls stacked with prayer beads, Buddha statues and saffron robes. Rickshaws rattled past. Monks walked barefoot, their robes bright against the dusty earth. Small monasteries from far-off nations dotted the town—Thailand's with its golden roofs, Japan's with its clean, angular lines, Tibet's festooned with prayer flags fluttering in the wind.

The temple glowed at night, its spire a beacon under strings of lights. Crickets sang, their chorus blending with distant chants. Ranji sat beneath the tree again, his silhouette framed by its branches, the crowd a quiet ring around him. I settled nearby, feeling the stillness.

'This place changes you,' I said, half to myself.

Neha, sitting cross-legged in the dark, replied, 'It's the tree. It holds the truth. You sit beneath it, you feel it.'

I nodded.

Ranji stayed only a day or two, but it felt like much longer. His presence drew pilgrims, journalists, children, monks. Stories bloomed: the barefoot president seeking Enlightenment, the man who gave up everything for silence. Vendors began calling out, 'Rice and milk for the quiet one!' their grins wide. Monks watched him, their chants softening as he passed. A boy ran up, his eyes wide. 'Does he talk to the tree?' he asked me, tugging my sleeve.

I smiled. 'Perhaps they talk to him,' I said, and the boy laughed, darting off to tell his friends.

The town pulsed with his legend, but Ranji remained silent, letting the tree and the temple speak. Bodh Gaya was a canvas—sacred, alive, ancient and urgent all at once. Ranji, barefoot and wordless, became a part of it for one quiet day, leaving behind only the sound of his steps and the weight of his stillness.

Chapter 24

Flowing Through India's Sacred Heart

The morning sun hung low over the horizon, spilling golden light across the rugged landscape as we trudged behind Ranji. His short, lean frame moved with a steady rhythm, barefoot as always, his simple white angavastram swaying with each step. We had been walking for days now. I, a co-traveller, scribbled notes in my worn notebook, trying to piece together the mystery of Ranji. Around us, the crowd swelled—men and women, young and old—their faces lit with curiosity, hope and something deeper, something I could not quite name.

Ranji had a way of pulling us along, not with words but with the quiet force of his presence. He carried no map, no plan that he shared, yet his path wove through the sacred heart of India like a thread stitching together a vast, ancient relic. He knew the dhams, the jyotirlingams, the Shakti sthals and the divya sthanams—holy places tied to the great epics, the Vedas and the Puranas. He led us to maths and ashrams, to hillocks carved with forgotten symbols, to shrines of every faith imaginable. His knowledge was not something he flaunted; it seeped out in the way he paused at a crumbling temple to trace its weathered stones with his fingers, or sat cross-legged beneath a banyan tree where yogis had meditated centuries ago. It was as if he had soaked up years of wandering, reading and listening, turning himself into a living book of wisdom.

I began to see a pattern in his steps. This was not just a walk; it was a pilgrimage, a search for something divine, something that tied all these places together. Ranji, like me, was a man of all faiths, rooted in a spirituality that ran deeper than any one religion. At times, he seemed almost atheist, detached from the rituals and chants that echoed around us. Yet there was a hunger in him, a longing to connect with the unseen force that held the world together. When he stopped at these sacred spots, he would sit, eyes closed, sinking into a stillness so complete it felt like the earth itself held its breath. Hours would pass, and he would remain there, unshaken by the heat, the dust or the crowd's growing hum. Once, long ago, he had whispered to me that every place had its own vibration—a pulse you could feel if you listened hard enough. I tried to join him, closing my eyes and reaching for that calm. But my mind buzzed like a restless fly, darting from thought to thought, never settling into the bliss that seemed to wrap Ranji like a second skin.

The crowds, though, saw something in him. To them, he was a saint, a sage, a figure of reverence. They pressed closer, hands outstretched for blessings, eyes wide with awe, hoping to catch his gaze or stand in his shadow. Ranji never flinched. He sat, serene and untouched, while I scrambled to manage the chaos. At first, it overwhelmed me—their voices, their pleading, the sheer weight of their numbers.

But then I stumbled on a trick. 'If you want to honour him,' I would call out, raising my voice above the din, 'clean this place. Make it worthy of his presence.'

And just like that, the energy shifted. Hands that had reached for Ranji now picked up brooms and buckets. Feet that had shuffled in restless devotion began sweeping away litter and dust. We became an army of *kar sevaks*, restoring temples, clearing paths, washing away years of neglect.

It was astonishing to watch. Entire towns transformed in the hours Ranji sat in meditation. A dusty shrine would gleam by midday, its steps scrubbed clean, its corners freed of cobwebs.

A littered street would turn spotless, the air fresher, the colours brighter. Even the pressmen who trailed us—pens poised for a story—and the security guards who grumbled about the crowds rolled up their sleeves and joined in. I would stand there, notebook in hand, marvelling at how Ranji's silence could stir such action. He never asked for it, never acknowledged it, but I think he knew. He trusted me to handle the worldly mess while he chased something higher.

One afternoon, we stopped at a small temple perched on a hill. Its stone walls were cracked, its courtyard overgrown with weeds, but there was a quiet power to it, a hum that prickled my skin. Ranji climbed the steps and settled beneath a pipal tree, its heart-shaped leaves rustling in the breeze. The crowd followed, spilling over the hillside, their murmurs rising like a tide. I spotted Neha and Arjun, two of our constant companions, weaving through the throng to reach me.

'This is getting bigger every day,' Neha said, wiping her forehead. 'How do you keep up?'

'I do not,' I admitted, grinning. 'They do it on their own now. Look.'

She followed my gaze to where a group of men pulled out vines from the temple walls, while women swept the courtyard with brisk, practised strokes. A boy, no older than ten, darted around with a basket, collecting scraps of paper and wilted flowers. Neha's eyes widened. 'You turned them into a cleaning crew?'

'It's the only offering they can give,' I said. 'Ranji does not want their prayers or their gifts. This keeps them busy, and it makes everything...better.'

Arjun squatted beside us, resting his chin in his hands. 'He is like a spark, is he not? He does not say a word, but everything catches fire around him.'

'Yes,' I said softly, watching Ranji's still form. 'A spark of something big.'

The day stretched on, and Ranji stayed beneath the tree, his breathing slow and even. The sun dipped lower, painting the sky in streaks of orange and pink. The crowd worked tirelessly, their chatter fading into a rhythm of effort. By dusk, the temple glowed; its stones freed of grime, its courtyard smooth and welcoming. Someone lit oil lamps along the steps, their flickering light dancing in the twilight. Ranji opened his eyes then, rising to his feet with a grace that silenced the air. He stepped forward, and the crowd parted, their faces glowing with pride at what they had accomplished.

As we walked away, Neha fell into step beside me. 'Do you ever wonder what he is searching for?' she asked, her voice low.

'All the time,' I said. 'He knows so much—every temple, every cave, every story. But it is more than that. It is like he is trying to feel it all, to touch something beyond us.'

Arjun glanced at Ranji, who walked ahead, his silhouette sharp against the fading light. 'Maybe he already has. Maybe that is why he does not talk.'

I did not have an answer, but the thought lingered. Ranji's journey was not merely about the places we visited; it was about the soul—his and ours. He stood for something pure, something that cut through the noise of the world. I had seen it when tough questions came up, when people pressed him about history's scars or the flaws we could not ignore. He never spoke, but his silence said everything. The soul, he seemed to believe, did not bend to fear or division. It stood with love, with freedom, with the spark of the human spirit that refused to be crushed.

One evening, we camped near a river, its waters glinting silver under the moon. Ranji sat on the bank, eyes closed, while the crowd buzzed around a fire they had built. I joined Neha and Arjun by the flames, warming my hands against the chill. The air smelled of smoke and wet earth, and the soft rush of the river filled the quiet.

'Today was different,' Neha said, poking at the fire with a stick. 'That village we passed through, they were arguing about some old feud. Land or something. They wanted Ranji to pick a side.'

I nodded, remembering the raised voices, the accusing fingers. 'He did not, though. He just sat there until they stopped shouting.'

Arjun laughed. 'And then they started cleaning the riverbank instead. How does he do that?'

'It is not him,' I said slowly. 'It is us. He makes us look at ourselves, and we figure out what matters.'

Neha tilted her head, the firelight flickering in her

eyes. 'Do you think he is teaching us without saying anything?'

'Maybe,' I said. 'Or perhaps he is just being, and we are the ones learning.'

The next morning, we reached a crumbling fort atop a hill, its walls etched with carvings of gods and warriors. Ranji climbed to the highest point and sat down, gazing out at the rolling plains below. The crowd swelled again, spilling across the slopes, their voices rising in a hum of excitement. I called out the familiar refrain, 'Clean this place!', and the inhabitants set to work, hauling away stones, sweeping dust, clearing the tangled brush. Security formed a loose ring around Ranji, keeping the eager ones at bay, while I scribbled notes, trying to capture the strange, beautiful chaos of it all.

By midday, the fort looked alive again, its ancient bones freed of neglect. Ranji stood, and the crowd stilled, watching him with a reverence that felt almost tangible. He began to walk, and we followed, down the hill and into the next stretch of the unknown. The sun set, the earth crunched beneath our feet, and I felt it again—that pull, that sense of purpose Ranji carried like a flame.

He was changing us, step by step. Towns grew cleaner, hearts grew lighter, and minds turned inward, sifting through clutter we did not even know we carried. Ranji, the silent enigma, was a mirror and a guide, showing us the soul's quiet strength. And as we walked, I knew this journey was far from over. There were more places to see, more lessons to learn, and a divinity waiting just beyond the horizon.

Chapter 25

Echoes of Faith and Fragile Waters

The salty breeze swept over us as we approached Rameswaram, an island cradled by the sea, its edges blurring into the waves. Ranji walked ahead, his bare feet pressing into the sandy earth, his white shirt catching the wind like a sail.

I followed closely, my notebook damp from the humid air, my heart stirring with a mix of awe and memory. Behind us, the crowd stretched long and wide, a river of people flowing with us, their voices a soft hum against the crash of the ocean. We had crossed the railway bridge earlier, its old iron frame rattling beneath our steps, pausing midway to let a ship glide through. We then walked the road bridge, its concrete firm and new, tying this sacred island to the mainland. Rameswaram felt like a world apart, where land and water danced together—fragile and fierce.

This was no ordinary stop. Rameswaram was one of the Char Dham, a pillar of Hindu pilgrimage, a place every devotee longed to touch. At its heart stood the Shiva temple, its towering gopuram piercing the sky, its stones whispering tales of Lord Rama. The Ramayana was alive here. They say Lord Rama knelt on this soil, praying to Lord Shiva before building the bridge to Lanka—the Rama Setu—to rescue Sita from Ravana. Even now, you could see traces of it: faint sand dunes drifting in the shallow waters, stretching towards the horizon where Jaffna lay. Ranji had brought us to this holy ground, and the weight of it settled over me like a cloak.

But the island was not only shrine. It cradled a marine national park, a biosphere reserve where the sea teemed with life. Corals glowed beneath the waves, fish darted in bright schools, turtles glided silently. The air buzzed with the cries of seabirds, their wings flapping against the sky as they swooped over the beaches. Yet this beauty was fragile, stained by the hands of man. The waters around Rameswaram were a battleground too. Fishermen, their boats bobbing on the tides, cast nets into both Indian and Sri Lankan seas, often crossing invisible lines. The Navy and Coast Guard loomed large, their vessels patrolling the coast, eyes sharp for trespassers. These fishermen—tough and weathered— sometimes paid dearly, caught by Lankan patrols and

ATULYA MISRA

locked away in foreign jails, their families left waiting on these shores.

Across the water, Sri Lanka burned with its own wounds. The civil war there, a long and brutal scar, sent ripples to Rameswaram. Refugees washed up here, their boats fragile, their faces hollowed by loss. The insurgency had torn their island apart, and its echoes reached us. Tales of violence, of razed villages and unmoored lives, spilled across the strait. The pain of Tamil brothers and sisters over there seeped into the fishermen's songs, into the prayers whispered in the temple. Rameswaram was not just a place of faith—it was a witness to a fractured world, its shores cradling both devotion and despair.

We reached the temple at dawn, the sky still a soft pink and gold. The crowd swelled around us, pilgrims from every corner of India, their voices rising in chant. Ranji led us inside, his silence a stark contrast to the clamour. The air was thick with incense, the stones cool beneath our feet. We followed the ritual: bathing in the waters of twenty-two wells, each step a washing, a surrender. The water was cold, tasting of salt and sand, and I shivered as it ran down my spine. Ranji moved through it all with quiet grace, his eyes distant, his hands steady as the priest poured the sacred water over him.

When we entered the sanctum for darshan, the world seemed to hush. The Shivalingam gleamed in the flickering light of oil lamps, its presence ancient and vast. I stood beside Ranji, my breath catching as the priests chanted, their voices weaving a thread of sound that bound us all. The crowd pressed close, their hands outstretched, their eyes wet with reverence. Ranji gazed at the lingam, unmoving, and I wondered what he saw—his family, his past, the souls he carried in silence.

Neha, ever curious, leaned towards me as we stepped outside. 'What do you think he is praying for?' she asked, her voice barely a whisper.

I glanced at Ranji, his figure framed against the temple's stone walls. 'Maybe for his parents,' I said. 'For their moksha. He has come so far. Perhaps this is his duty as a son.'

Arjun joined us, his face flushed from the heat. 'Or maybe it's bigger than that. This place—it's tied to Lord Rama, to war, to rescue. Maybe he feels all of it.'

'Could be,' I said, my thoughts drifting to the sand dunes, the fragile bridge to Lanka. 'He's always chasing something we cannot see.'

After darshan, Ranji turned towards Dhanushkodi, the ghost town at the island's edge. We followed, the crowd thinning as the path grew rough. The ruins rose around us: crumbled walls of a railway station, a church half swallowed by sand, deserted quarters where officials once lived. A cyclone had swept through long ago, tearing it all apart, leaving only a shadow of what had been. I had been here before, years ago, scattering mud from my wife's village in Vietnam into the sea, a stand-in for her ashes. The memory stung, sharp and sudden, and

I blinked it away as Ranji stopped at the shore.

The three seas met here, their waters swirling in a dance of colours. Ranji bent down, cupping the waves in his hands, lifting them to the sky. His lips moved faintly—a prayer too soft to hear. I imagined it was for his father, his mother, his ancestors; a pind daan, an offering for the soul's peace. The crowd watched, hushed, their faces mirroring my own mix of wonder and ache. Many of them repeated the gesture and prayed.

Then, without warning, Ranji leapt into the sea. The water splashed around him as he swam—strong, swift—heading for the sand dunes that marked the Rama Setu. My heart lurched. 'Excellency!' I shouted, plunging in after him. The crowd erupted, some wading in, others calling out. Neha and Arjun splashed beside me, our legs churning through the shallow waves.

'Stop him!' Neha cried, her voice tight with panic. 'He's going too far!'

We swam and stumbled, the water dragging at us, the dunes slipping closer then farther as the tide pulled. Ranji reached one, climbed it, then dove back in, aiming for the next. I spotted Coast Guard boats in the distance, their engines roaring to life. Beyond them, Sri Lankan patrol ships loomed—dark shapes on the horizon. If he crossed that line, it would be more than danger—it would be a crisis.

'Excellency, please!' I shouted again, my throat raw. 'Come back!'

He did not hear, or did not care. The crowd's cries grew frantic, a chorus of fear. Then the hovercraft surged in, slicing through the waves, its crew hauling Ranji aboard just before he reached Lankan waters. Relief flooded me. My legs gave way as I sank into the shallows. The crowd cheered, their voices ragged and breathless, as the boat brought him back.

We gathered on the beach, wet and shaken. Ranji stood there, dripping, eyes fixed on the sea. Neha grabbed my arm. 'Why did he do that? What was he chasing?'

'I do not know,' I said, my voice unsteady. 'Maybe Rama's path. Maybe the pain over there. The war, the Tamils. He never tells us.'

Arjun shook his head, water streaming from his hair. 'He's an enigma. Always will be.'

A Coast Guard officer approached us, his face stern. 'You need to keep him in check. That could have gone bad—real bad.'

'I am sorry,' I said, my hands raised. 'He does not listen. He just...goes.'

The officer sighed, eyeing Ranji. 'Keep him on land next time. Please.'

We nodded, but I knew it was a promise I could not keep. Ranji was a force, wild and free, pulled by something deeper than we could touch. As the sun dipped low, casting gold across the waves, we walked back through Dhanushkodi's ruins. The national park stretched nearby, its corals and fish hidden beneath the surface, its fragility a quiet warning. The Sethusamudram project lingered too—a dream of cutting a channel for ships, stalled by debates over the Rama Setu, its sacred dunes, and the life they sheltered. Progress clashed with faith and nature here, and Ranji seemed to feel all of it.

That night, we camped on the shore, the sea's roar our lullaby. The crowd huddled close, their faces lit by a small fire. Neha stared into the flames. 'This place is so beautiful, but so broken. The war, the fishermen, the park...it is all hanging by a thread.'

'Yes,' I said, my eyes on Ranji, who sat apart, gazing at the sea. 'And he is walking through it as if he is trying to hold it together.'

Arjun tossed a stick into the fire. 'Or to understand it. Maybe that is why he swam out there...to feel what is across the sea.'

'Perhaps,' I said, my chest tight. 'But we will never know for sure.'

The stars glittered above. The waves whispered their secrets. And Ranji sat in silence, his journey unfolding before us like the tides—endless, unknowable, and alive with purpose.

Chapter 26

Through the Shadows of a Changing Land

The sun was barely up, a faint glow creeping over the horizon, when we set out behind Ranji once more. He led the way, barefoot as always, his angavastram fluttering in the early breeze. I walked close behind, my notebook tucked under my arm, my eyes tracing the path he carved through the dust. Around us, the crowd grew—a shifting sea of faces, some familiar, some new, all drawn to this man who had risen from his pyre and begun a journey no one fully understood. We were a strange caravan moving through India's vast, wounded heart, our steps echoing with stories of loss and endurance.

Ranji's path led us through places most would rather forget. We passed towns hollowed by mining—hillsides ripped open, rivers clogged with silt. We walked through lands swallowed by dams, where whole villages had vanished beneath water, their people shuffled off to resettlement colonies—rows of concrete boxes with no soul. We entered refugee camps, their tents sagging in the wind, filled with families displaced by conflict, their eyes dulled by grief. There were cemeteries too, silent and orderly, where soldiers lay beneath neat stones, and wastelands where landslides or earthquakes had swept away homes, leaving nothing but scars on the earth.

The people we met in these places carried a shared weariness. They were unmoored, rootless, their pasts dissolved. You could see it in their faces—creases deepened by time, eyes clouded with a pain that stretched across generations. Their children played in the dust, their laughter quick and piercing, as if they had inherited the ache without understanding it. These were the sacrificed—the ones modern India had cast aside for mines, for dams, for the shining towers of its new cities. Their voices had been silenced, their stories erased in the name of progress. Many had ended up in the slums—those crowded, chaotic places that belonged to no one and everyone.

The slums were alive in a way that was both beautiful and brutal. One morning, we stepped into one thick with the scent of smoke, sweat, and garbage. Narrow lanes twisted between shacks patched together from tin, tarp and hope. Houses leaned against each other, their walls thin as paper, their roofs sagging under the weight of time. Children darted through the alleys, chasing each other with sticks. Women crouched over buckets, scrubbing clothes in murky water from a shared tap. Men sat in doorways—hammering metal, stitching torn cloth—their hands moving with a rhythm born of necessity. Everywhere, life pulsed messy, loud and unyielding.

Garbage heaps rose like small hills, buzzing with flies, spilling into the lanes. A sluggish drainage ditch snaked along the side, thick and black. A single community toilet stood at the end of a row, its door hanging loose. Tiny temples, mosques, and churches squeezed between the shacks their bells and prayers drifting into the smoke. Some homes doubled as workshops: sewing machines whirring, plastic bags rustling, the air sharp with the tang of solder. Others were makeshift shops, shelves stuffed with cigarettes, sweets and packets of soap. Quacks peddled remedies, tuition centres clung to fading signs, and boys lifted rusted weights in a one-room gym, their grunts echoing in the gloom. It was a world stacked on itself—every inch claimed, every breath shared.

Ranji walked through it all, his steps slow and deliberate. The crowd pressed close, murmuring, but he remained untouched by the noise. Then, something shifted. An old man stumbled from a doorway, his eyes widening when they met Ranji's. 'You,' he rasped, his voice trembling. 'I never thought...' He reached out, and Ranji stopped, turning to him. The man's hands shook as he grasped Ranji's, and for a long moment, they stood there, silent, as if the years between them melted away.

I stepped closer, curiosity pulling me in. 'Who is he?' I asked a woman nearby, her arms loaded with wet laundry.

She glanced over. Her face softened. 'Old friend, maybe. Ranji has been here before, long ago. People say he lived with us once, shared our rice, slept on our floors.'

Ranji sat, gently pulling the man down beside him. They remained like that, hand in hand, eyes closed. The crowd quieted. I felt a lump rise in my throat—it was as though they had reached back into the past and found something that still lived, warm and real.

'It is like he is collecting threads, weaving them back together,' Neha remarked, her voice low.

Arjun joined us. 'Makes you wonder how many lives he has touched. How many stories he carries in that silence.'

'Too many to count,' I said, watching Ranji and the old man. 'And he never says a word.'

The day wore on, and Ranji rose, moving deeper into the slum. The crowd followed, their numbers swelling, their voices a constant hum. I called out, 'Clean this place!', my usual trick, and they sprang into action. Brooms appeared, hands scooped up trash, and soon the lanes began to breathe again. Even the kids pitched in, giggling as they hauled buckets of dirt to the dump. It was chaos turned to purpose, and I stood back, scribbling notes, marvelling at how Ranji's silence could spark such change.

Later, we sat near a water tank. The surface was filmed with grime, green and oily. Neha dipped her fingers in and recoiled. 'This is disgusting! So filthy. How do they live like this?'

'They do not have a choice,' I said. 'The waste just piles up. No one comes to take it away.'

Arjun kicked at a nearby heap of plastic bags. 'Ranji cares about this, doesn't he? The dirt, the mess.'

'He does,' I said. 'He's always looking at it, like he is trying to figure out how to fix it.'

Ranji was passionate about the waste, the heaps of garbage that shadowed every corner of India. In the slums, it was worse: mountains of trash, unsegregated, rotting in the open. Flies swarmed, rats scurried and the air grew thick with sickness. People lived alongside it, their children playing in its shadow, their homes pressed against its stench. Ranji knew this was not just a small problem. It was a beast, too big for brooms and buckets. Technology was the answer, he seemed to believe, though he never said it. Machines to sort, burn, recycle. But for now, all we had were our hands, and so we swept and hauled, a temporary balm on a gaping wound.

That night, we camped at the slum's edge, the sky above dark and starless, choked by the haze of city fumes. A fire crackled between us, casting long shadows on the crowd's weary faces. Neha sat beside me, drawing her shawl closer. 'These people...they have lost so much. Their homes, their roots. And now this.'

'True,' I said, staring into the flames. 'But they keep going. They build something out of nothing.'

Arjun leaned in, his eyes serious. 'Ranji sees that, doesn't he? That strength.'

'I think so,' I said. 'He does not see just the pain. He sees the fight in them.'

The next day, we moved on, leaving the slum behind but carrying its weight with us. Ranji led us to a mining town next, its air thick with dust, its hills scarred and hollow. The people there were the same: displaced, lost, their lives reshaped by forces they could not control. Ranji found another friend, a woman this time, her hands rough from years of labour. They sat together, silent, while the crowd cleaned the streets, their brooms kicking up clouds of grit.

As the sun melted into the evening, painting the sky in streaks of red, I watched Ranji rise and walk on; the crowd followed. My legs ached, my heart was heavy, but there was something else too: a flicker of awe. These places, these people, they were the shadows of India's march forward, the ones left behind. And Ranji, in his quiet way, was shining a light on them, pulling us into their world, making us see. We were more than travellers now; we were witnesses, swept up in a journey that stitched together the broken pieces of a land still fighting to hold on.

Chapter 27

The Last Cry beneath
the Lone Pine

The air was thick with the scent of earth and leaves as we reached the Kurangani Hills, a rugged stretch straddling Tamil Nadu and Kerala. The sun hung low, casting long shadows over the rolling slopes, and Ranji strode ahead, his bare feet pressing into the soil with a purpose I had not seen before. I followed, clutching my notebook, my heart pounding with a mix of exhaustion and wonder. Behind us, the crowd swelled—thousands now—a sea of men, women and youth who had walked with us across India, drawn to this silent man who had risen from his pyre and led us on a journey none could fully comprehend.

The media buzzed like flies, their cameras flashing, their voices shouting questions into the wind. Security trailed us too, faces tense, hands hovering near their weapons. But Ranji paid them no mind. He was climbing now—slow at first, then faster—his frail frame moving towards the peak where a single pine tree stood.

I knew this place was special to him. Kurangani was his beginning, his root. He'd been born here, an orphan scraping by in these wild hills, a boy with no family but the forest. He had grown up among these trees, learned their secrets, and later became an ecotourism guide, leading wanderers through the green maze. It was here, years ago, that he had faced the fire, a roaring beast that swept through the hills, swallowing everything in its path. Ranji had run into the flames and saved eleven girls, pulling them out from the blaze. One of them was Radha, a girl he had carried on his back as the heat licked at his heels. I could still see the tension in his face, as if the reel of that day kept playing behind his eyes.

The village hailed him a hero, but fate had been cruel. It landed him in jail as a scapegoat. Yet his spirit held firm. An enquiry and testimony cleared his name of all false accusations. They gave him a civilian bravery award, a medal that gleamed briefly before he moved on, becoming a forester, guarding the wild he loved. Life pulled him higher still, against all odds, until he rose to become President of India—a quiet man in a loud world. And then, one day, he walked away from it all, rising from his pyre to begin this pilgrimage, a journey that had led him back here, to where it all began.

The hills rose steep and untamed around us,

their slopes blanketed in thick vegetation. Grasses swayed golden in the breeze, dotted with shrubs and wildflowers—purple bursts of kurinji and red splashes of flame lilies. Teak and sandalwood stretched tall, their bark rough and dry, while bamboo thickets rustled like whispers in the wind. This was elephant country too—a corridor where the giants roamed free, their paths worn deep into the soil. You could feel their presence in the snapped branches, the trampled grass, the faint rumble that lingered beneath your feet.

And there, at the top, stood that lone pine tree—a stranger in this land of broadleaves and grasses, planted by some unknown tea planter for reasons long forgotten. It thrived here, alien but unyielding, its needles sharp and green, its roots clawing into the slope. It was a survivor, like Ranji—standing apart yet offering shade to all: deer resting beneath it, langurs napping in its shadow, even the wind finding peace in its branches. When the fire broke out, it had shielded those who clung to its base.

Ranji climbed faster now, his breath coming in gasps, and the crowd surged behind him. The Forest Department officials scrambled, their voices crackling over radios, their men racing to block the paths. 'Stay back!' they shouted, waving batons, but the people pressed on—a tide too strong to contain. Police joined in, their boots pounding, faces flushed with panic.

Ranji turned then, his hands folding in a silent plea. Do not follow me, he gestured. His eyes met mine, sharp and clear, and I felt a jolt. He wanted me to stop too. Reluctantly, I sank on to a stone, my legs trembling, my chest tight from sheer fatigue. The security detail hesitated, then stepped back, their guns lowering. Ranji climbed alone. I watched his shrinking form, a speck against the vast green canvas, heading for the pine.

The crowd fell silent, eyes fixed on him. The media whispered into microphones, their lenses zoomed in. I squinted, heart racing, as he neared the tree. Its branches swayed gently in the breeze, a green flame in the fading light.

And then it happened—a sound tore through the air, raw and wild. It was not human. Not animal. Something else. A long, piercing cry that rose and fell, echoing off the hills, bouncing back in waves. Ranji's mouth was open, chest heaving, and the sound poured out of him—a symphony of grief and triumph, a stereophonic howl that filled the sky. The hills became an amphitheatre, amplifying every note, every wail, until the air itself seemed to tremble.

I leapt to my feet, my pulse roaring in my ears. 'Excellency!' I shouted, running towards him, my notebook forgotten. The security stirred, their boots thudding behind me, their voices yelling at Ranji to stop. And then I saw it—a sight so vast, so impossible, it stole my breath.

From the scrub below, elephants emerged—grey hides glinting in the dusk. First a few, then dozens, then hundreds coming from behind the trees, their trunks raised, their feet shaking the earth. They answered Ranji's call—deep rumbles, sharp trumpets, a chorus that drowned the world.

The herd surged towards the pine—males with tusks gleaming, females guiding calves—moving as one. The ground quaked, dust rose in clouds. They came from every direction, streaming over hillocks, bursting through bamboo, an army drawn to their master. Ranji stood beneath the pine, his frail body bathed in the last rays of the sun, a golden glow that turned him into something more than human. The elephants surrounded him, their trunks curling, their ears flapping, their cries a joyful storm. Calves danced around his legs, nudging him with tiny snouts, while a massive bull lifted him gently, placing him on its back.

Ranji sat there, a king without a crown, his hands stroking the beast's rough hide, his face alight with a peace I had never seen.

A helicopter circled, its light blinding, but it could not land. The elephants were too many and too close. The pilot veered off, shouting into his radio for explosives, for backup, for options. The security detail froze at the edge of the herd, their jaws slack, their fear melting into awe. I pushed closer, tears stinging my eyes, my voice lost in the roar.

The sun slipped behind a distant hill, its final rays painting the pine in orange and gold, and then darkness fell, swift and deep. The elephants turned, moving back towards the forest, Ranji riding high. They were taking him, claiming him, their lost brother found. I ran after them, my legs burning, my cries swallowed by the night, but they were gone, swallowed by the trees, their rumbles fading into silence.

The pine stood alone once more, its silhouette stark in the searchlights that swept the hill. The crowd broke free, shattering the barriers, a flood of bodies scrambling up the steep slope. Marshals shouted, their voices hoarse, as people slipped and fell, their hands clawing at the earth. Light bombs flared, lighting up the sky, then fading back to black. The stars blazed overhead—Saptarishi, Orion's belt, Mars a dull red speck—watching over us on this new moon night. I sank to my knees, my chest heaving, my hands empty.

Ranji was gone. The security milled around, useless now, their torches flickering. The media swarmed, their questions a dull buzz in my ears.

Neha found me, her face streaked with dirt and tears. 'Where is he?' she whispered, her voice breaking. 'What just happened?'

'He is gone,' I said, my voice raw. 'The elephants... they took him.'

Arjun stumbled over, his eyes wide with shock. 'That sound—he called them. They knew him.'

'Yes,' I said, my gaze fixed on the pine. 'This was his home. His real home.'

The night stretched on, cold and endless. Army battalions arrived, their boots crunching the grass, their orders sharp in the dark. Foresters poured in from nearby ranges, their faces grim, their lanterns swinging. Firemen, police, revenue officials, they all came, a desperate army hunting for a man who had vanished into the wild. Searchlights swept the hills, helicopters hovered, but the forest held its silence. Days passed. The search slowed. The world moved on. But we couldn't.

One early morning, I sat beneath the pine one last time, its needles whispering in the breeze, its shade cool against my skin. Dawn was yet to break. The crowd had thinned, the media had drifted away. Only Neha and Arjun stayed with me, their presence a quiet anchor. The hill was scarred now, trampled by feet and machines, but the pine stood tall, untouched by the chaos. It had seen Ranji's life unfold: his lonely childhood, his courage in the fire, his hidden love for Radha, his rise and fall and rise again. It had watched him climb, heard his cry, welcomed him home. And now it stood as his witness, a green sentinel in a world he had left behind.

'He was one of them,' Neha said, her voice soft, her eyes on the tree. 'The elephants knew it all along.'

'Yeah,' I said, my fingers tracing the pine's rough bark. 'He belonged here, with the wild.'

Arjun sat beside us, his head in his hands. 'He saved those girls, saved the forest, saved us in a way. And then he just...went back to it.'

I nodded, tears spilling down my cheeks. 'He was the pine tree, was he not? Alone, different, but strong. Surviving where he did not belong, giving shade to everyone.'

The wind rustled through the needles, and I closed my eyes, letting the sound wash over me. Ranji's journey had woven through India's heart—its slums, its temples, its broken lands, its sacred hills. He had shown us its beauty and its pain, its strength and its fragility, all without a word. From an orphan in these hills to the President of India, he had carried Kurangani with him, a piece of wilderness in his soul. And now, he had returned. Not as a man, but something more—a cry in the wind, a shadow among the elephants, a memory etched into this lone pine.

We sat there, the three of us, as the sun rose, its light spilling over the hills once more. The forest stretched below, alive with birdsong and rustling leaves, the elephant corridors hidden but pulsing with life. Ranji was gone, but his echo lingered, in the pine's green crown, in the earth beneath our feet, in the hearts of those who had walked beside him. He had climbed this hill to end his journey, not with a whisper, but with a roar that shook the world. As the light grew, I knew this was his farewell—a dramatic, blazing thread tying all his steps together, a final gift to the land that had shaped him, and to us, who had followed him to the end.

Epilogue

The land remembers.
The lone pine remembers.
The silent hills remember.

He is no longer a man with feet of dust.
He is the cry in the wind,
the echo beneath the earth,
the shadow near the river's bend.

He has slipped beyond the reach of names,
beyond the grasp of time.
He has become what he always was:
Witness, fire and soul.

And those who walked with him—
those who loved, feared, doubted and believed—
carry him still.

In their steps.
In their dreams.
In the testimony that will never be silenced.

The journey does not end.
It only changes form.

Acknowledgements

My heartfelt thanks to Rupa Publications for their meticulous work in refining and publishing this book. I am also profoundly grateful to my personal staff—especially Vijayaprabha, Premkumar and Kannabiran—for their quiet dedication and support.

To my friends Ranjeet, Anurag, Akash, and my aunt Nirupama, thank you for your thoughtful suggestions and encouragement throughout this journey.

Above all, I express my deepest gratitude to my wife, Pallavi, and to my children, Ayush, Indrani and Ishita, for their constant encouragement and belief in me.

www.ingramcontent.com/pod-product-compliance
Lightning Source LLC
Chambersburg PA
CBHW020346100426
42812CB00035B/3377/J